Charles Bray

On force, its mental and moral correlates

On that which is supposed to underlie all phenomena: with speculations on spiritualism and other abnormal conditions of mind

Charles Bray

On force, its mental and moral correlates
On that which is supposed to underlie all phenomena: with speculations on spiritualism and other abnormal conditions of mind

ISBN/EAN: 9783741144882

Manufactured in Europe, USA, Canada, Australia, Japa

Cover: Foto ©Thomas Meinert / pixelio.de

Manufactured and distributed by brebook publishing software (www.brebook.com)

Charles Bray

On force, its mental and moral correlates

ON FORCE,

ITS
MENTAL AND MORAL CORRELATES;

AND ON THAT WHICH IS
SUPPOSED TO UNDERLIE ALL PHENOMENA:
WITH SPECULATIONS ON SPIRITUALISM,
AND OTHER ABNORMAL CONDITIONS OF MIND.

BY CHARLES BRAY,

AUTHOR OF THE "PHILOSOPHY OF NECESSITY," THE "EDUCATION OF THE FEELINGS," ETC.

"He who, believing that the search for truth can never be offensive to the God of truth, pursues his way with an unswerving energy, may not unreasonably hope that he may assist others in their struggle towards the light, and may in some small degree contribute to that consummation when the professed belief shall have been adjusted to the requirements of the age, when the old tyranny shall have been broken, and the anarchy of transition shall have passed away."—*Lecky's History of Rationalism.*

"In the present state of science, of all subjects that on which we know least is, perhaps, the connection of our bodily and mental nature, the action of the one on the other," &c.—*Professor the Rev. Baden Powell.*

"Metaphysics revolve in an endless circle of abstractions, rhino have scarcely made any permanent advance since the introduction of Christianity." —*Times, January 1st, 1866.*

"All our conceptions are based on the implied postulate that the world is as it appears. * * * The advance of knowledge consists in the substitution of accurate conceptions for natural ones."—*Man and his Dwelling Place, by James Hinton.*

"It remains for philosophers to place Physiology and Mental and Moral Philosophy in the same position as positive sciences reached by induction."— *H. G. Atkinson, F.G.S.*

"Men rarely recount facts simply as they happened, but mingle their own opinions with them; more especially if the facts are above their comprehension, and connected with religious interests."—*Spinoza.*

"There are few delusions that a man cannot be brought to believe if they injure neither his stomach nor his purse."—*Times, April 27th, 1863.*

"If the Critic speaks, it is not to tell the reader what the Philosopher thinks, but what he thinks of the Philosopher: a quite uninteresting matter." —*Fortnightly Review.*

LONDON:
LONGMANS, GREEN, READER, AND DYER.

THE RIGHT OF TRANSLATION IS RESERVED.

PREFACE.

THE doctrine of Philosophical Necessity, notwithstanding its supposed horrible tendency to sap the foundation of morals, has been elevated from the regions below, where, according to Milton, its discussion furnished fit occupation and amusement for devils only,—to form the base of Social Science. Philosophical Necessity is only another name for "Law" or a fixed order of Nature in the department of Mind, and there can be no Social *Science* without it. This I have endeavoured to make plain in my work on "The Philosophy of Necessity," and it is my purpose now to show that the doctrine of the Correlation and Persistence of Forces, when thought out to its legitimate consequences, gives us a Science of Psychology based on Physiology, by which alone we can attain to the same command over mind, as we already have over physical force. The Irishman's direction for making a cannon, "Take a long hole, and pour metal round it," has been followed by Metaphysicians in making their *canons*, and the "method" has produced results such as might have been expected. Consciousness, their round hole, has no substantial existence out of the individual mind reflecting upon it, and it is difficult to pour metal round it, and the canons so founded result only in the *ipse dixit* of the founder, which every succeeding philosopher thinks is necessary to burst before he proceeds to cast any of his own. Mind is force, and it must be studied as all other forces are, as well as by "reflection on consciousness," and then Metaphysics may take the place to which it is entitled at the head of all other Sciences.

The Correlation of Forces shows that in the cycle of forces we can always return to the same starting point without a break, and the Persistence of Force shows that this is always done without loss; now these truths, not stopping short in Physics, but carried, as they ought to be, into the higher field of Mind, furnish, I think, the most probable explanation of "the Phenomena of Modern Spiritualism," at the present time so much puzzling earnest investigators. My speculations however are given only as speculations; I have no wish to dogmatise, I merely present an hypothesis to be rejected or affirmed by observation and experience. History now has shown that we must not be deterred from the acceptance of any truth from its supposed consequences. Friar Bacon was cast into prison as a magician by the Superior of his Order, and the mysteries of physical science were treated then very much as the mysteries of mental science are now. Mr.

Lowes says, (*Fortnightly Review*, Feb. 1, 1866), "We are warned against Materialism as cold and desolating. The real warning should be against materialism as erroneous; in point of fact, we do not find materialists are cold and desolated, any more than spiritualists are hot and happy." We must not ask then, "To what will this lead? but is it true?" No truth is really at variance with other truth, and if it should appear to be so, we must be content to wait till we understand the whole matter. We are not bound, however, to attach every new truth to some old error or superstition and then wait till we can reconcile the two, before we reason it out to its legitimate consequences: this would be to make it powerless and inoperative. Thus Professor Mansel, in the *Contemporary Review*, No. 5, for May, 1860, says, "Eternity and continuous duration — immutability and creation in time — perfect action, yet unexhausted power to act — everlasting purpose and accessibility to prayer — general law and special providence — complete fore-knowledge co-existing with human freedom, — we cannot combine these several elements together into a consistent whole, yet we can believe that they are capable of combination:" but I confess I find in myself no such wonderful power of belief; on the contrary, the propositions appear to me as contradictory as that a thing may be and may not be at the same time. Some of the propositions may lie beyond our depth, but I certainly cannot conceive how an occurrence can be fore-known which is contingent, that is, if man is really free, may happen or may not happen; neither do I feel myself called upon to believe in any such freedom, for if it really existed it would completely paralyse man's action,—as there could be no prevision either in God or man.

This short Treatise is dedicated to those, and to those only, who love truth above all things, for its own sake.

CONTENTS.

	PAGE
CHAPTER I.—On Force	1
CHAPTER II.—Force; its Mental Correlates	7
Section 1. The Psychology of Phrenology	23
Section 2. The Persistence of Force	35
CHAPTER III.—Upon that which Underlies all Phenomena	47
CHAPTER IV.—Speculations on Spiritualism and other Abnormal Conditions of Mind	69

The Correlation of Force in Living Structures.—Matter and Spirit the same in Essence.—Time and Space.—The Correlation of the Vital and Mental Forces.—The Conditions attending Influx or Inspiration.—Memory.

SPIRITUALISM.—Genuineness of the Phenomena.—Application of the Theory: Physical Force, Table Moving, Rapping, Levitation, &c.—Intelligence.—Investigators into Spiritual Manifestations who have rejected the Notion of Spirits.—History Confirms the Existence of the Phenomena.—The Manifestations in the Catholic Church.—Witchcraft.—The Abnormal Mental Powers of the Founders of Sects.—The Constitution of the Medium.—The Spirits; their Abodes and Occupations.—The Rationale of the Spiritual Phenomena.—The Coming Spirit World evolved from the Spirit Atmosphere, the result of Cerebration.

ARGUMENT.

There is but one thing known to us in the universe; this, Physical Philosophers have called "Force." The Reality or Entity underlying it, or that of which it is the Force, Metaphysicians have called "Noumenon." It is the "Substance" of Spinoza, and the "Being" of Hegel.

Everything around us results from the mode of action or motion, or correlation of this one force, the different Forms of which we call Phenomena.

The difference in the mode of action depends upon the difference in the Structure it passes through; each Structure consisting of concentrated Force, or centres of Force, and has been called Matter. "Every form is force visible; a form of rest is a balance of forces; a form undergoing change is the predominance of one over others."—*Huxley*.

Heat, Light, Magnetism, Electricity, Attraction, Repulsion, Chemical Affinity, Life, Mind or Sentience, are modes of action or manifestations of Force, and die or cease to exist when the Force passes on into other forms.

Cause and Effect form this sequence or correlation; and each cause and effect is a new Life and a new Death: each form being a new creation, which dies and passes away, never to return; for "nothing repeats itself, because nothing can be placed again in the same condition; the past being irrevocable."—*W. R. Grove*. "There is no death in the concrete, what passes away passes away into its own self—only the passing away passes away."—*Hegel*.

Force passing through a portion of the structure of the brain, creates the "World" of our intellectual consciousness, with the "ego," or sense of personal identity; passing through other portions the world of our likes and antipathies—called the Moral world; Good and Evil being purely subjective.

The character and direction of Volition depend upon the Persistent Force and the structure through which it passes. Every existing state, both bodily and mental, has grown out of the preceding, and all its Forces have been used up in present phenomena. Thus, "everything that exists depends upon the past, prepares the future, and is related to the whole."—*Oersted*.

As no force acts singly, but is always combined with other forces or modes of action to produce some given purpose or particular result, we infer that Force is not blind but intelligent; as it is One, we infer it is the force of an Intelligent Being—possessing personality; and that Being we have called God. "He is the universal Being of which all things are the manifestations."—*Spinoza*.

All force or power is Will power,—the will of God. "Causation is the will, Creation the act of God."—*W. R. Grove*. The will which originally required a distinct conscious volition has passed, in the ages, into the unconscious or automatic, constituting the fixed laws and order of nature.

Vital Force exists in excess in some constitutions, and may be transferred to other living organisms, often constituting a curative agent.

Brain Force, the result of cerebration, also exists in excess in some nervous constitutions; it then forms a sphere or atmosphere around individuals by which one brain is brought into communication with others and mind becomes a unity. Individual will-power can act through this medium beyond the range of individual body. In this way may be explained the Mysteries of Magic and Witchcraft, the Phenomena of Mesmerism, of so-called Spiritualism, and the Curative Power of Individuals.

ERRATA.

"There is nothing underlying phenomena—phenomena are correlates of force, and force is all," p. 48. By this the author simply means that motion cannot be separated from the thing moving, or force or power be delegated, or separated from that which it is the force of,—that is, the source of all power. "God's power," as Spinoza says, "is the same as his essence," and all change therefore is but "the varied God." Properties, qualities, or attributes, are powers, and when said to exist per se, it is in the same sense. They have no separate existence, and are therefore untransferable.

For "emotion," p. 14, line 4, read "motion."
For "perception," p. 14, line 7, read "succession;" and for "pass," same line, read "passes."
For "heaps," p. 47, line 3, read "harps."
In p. 67, line 3, "if" is omitted.
For "assume," p. 71, line 17, read "issuate."
For "figures," p. 86, line 21, read "forms."
For "anthropological," p. 88, line 27, read "anthropomorphical."
For "Tyara," p. 117, line 11, read "Tyana."
For "to," p. 128, last line but one, read "have been."
For "lectation," p. 129, line 8, read "lactation."

FORCE, AND ITS MENTAL AND MORAL CORRELATES.

CHAPTER I.

ON FORCE.

NOT very long ago all the world believed that the sun went round the earth; they saw that it did; now all the world (with a very small exception) believes in the existence of matter; they see it, they feel it, and that is enough. But paradoxical as it may seem, philosophers, after the most diligent research have failed to find matter anywhere, and whereas we were wont to speak of the impenetrability and indestructibility of matter, we now speak only of the persistence and conservation or indestructibility of Force. The assumption that the force which acts upon us, and of which only therefore we know anything, belongs to something else which we call matter, is gratuitous, unwarrantable, and altogether unnecessary. Heat and Light were until very recently thought to be matter, but the material theory with respect to those is now given up. Count Rumford boiled water by thumping upon iron, and Sir Humphrey Davy produced heat by rubbing two pieces of ice together. As concussion and friction therefore produced heat, heat was thought to be not matter, but motion. But motion is *nothing*,—It is the mere mode of action of Force and the transference of it in greater or less intensity, from one point of space to another. The heat from friction and arrested motion is merely an illustration of the persistence of force, of its varying action in different conditions, and of the transference of it from one centre of force (which we call body) to another. Heat and Light are the same, that is, different modes of action or motion of the same force, as are also electricity, magnetism, and chemical affinity; that is to say, they are correlates, and all change readily into each other without loss of quantity of the original Force. These forces, or rather this force, since all are convertible, is the source of the delusion we are under with respect to matter, when we say we see and feel it. For what do we see? Light, which is force, photographs a minute inverted image on the bottom of the eye—on the retina, which acting on the Brain produces consciousness of an object. All that is known to us is the mental conception,—the *reality* of which our conception is composed is Force. It is evident there is no matter here. But surely we feel matter if we do not see it? The sense of Feeling is mere repulsion—resistance to motion. When we speak of matter as subtle, or as solid, liquid, or aeriform, we simply mean that it presents more or less resistance to motion. "When the question arises," says J. S. Mill, "whether something which affects our senses in a peculiar way, as for instance whether Heat or Light, or Electricity, is, or is not matter, what seems always to be meant is, does it offer any, however trifling, resistance to motion? If it were shown that it did, this would at once terminate all doubt." But Resistance is repulsion or force, which acting on the sense causes a sensation; when acting on the brain, an idea.

In Chemistry we find only circles or centres of force —the ultimate atoms, which this force is supposed to surround, are an uncalled for and altogether unnecessary invention. When I speak of body therefore or substance, I mean these circles of force in a more or less intense or condensed condition. The way in which force acts depends upon its relation to these bodies, or what have been called "potential energies"; going in at one end of a row of billiard balls it comes out at the other, with little or no change even in quantity, but it varies according to the complexity of the substance or organization through which it passes, that is, to the relation it bears to previously arranged forces. But when we speak of either matter or force we speak only of the external cause of our sensations and ideas, and these tell us nothing of the real nature or essence of either; why not then continue to use the term matter as heretofore? We answer because the more general term force may include and does really include both what has hitherto been called Matter and Spirit also. We are told that "Force viewed separately from matter is nothing." I think it more correct to say that matter viewed separately from force is nothing, because we know that force passes into or changes into mind, as heat into light, and we thus include both sides of creation—Matter and Spirit. Force, in its different modes of action as Light, Heat, Electricity, Galvanism, Chemical Affinity, Attraction and Repulsion, is sufficient to produce half the phenomena around us. Life and Mind, which are correlates of Force, or other modes of its action, are sufficient to produce the other half. There is but One simple, primordial, absolute Force, with varying relations and conditions. The modes of Force or Effects now in existence are neither more nor less than such as have previously existed, changed only in form. They have not merely acted upon each other, according to the common supposition with respect to matter, BUT HAVE CHANGED INTO EACH OTHER. This will be found to be a very important distinction. Each change is a new creation of something which in that form or mode has never existed before—a new life, and as it passes into another form or mode, a new death—"nothing repeats itself, because nothing can be placed again in the same condition: the past is irrevocable." * And may we not add irrecoverable.

Motion or change is constantly producing new relations and conditions. We cannot speak of motion as existing by itself, as it is merely a mode of action of Force, and Force therefore cannot be separated from it, but must always attend it; the same may be said of all the Imponderables, which are mere modes of action, or Force in motion. It is in this way, probably, that Force itself escapes us, because it is only with its modes or motions that we have to do: for we know nothing of Force in itself, we know it only by its effects, and when we say therefore that something takes place by the force of attraction, repulsion, electrical or chemical affinity, &c., we only mean that a certain group of phenomena occur in a certain order, and that they occur uniformly and invariably in that order.

Cause and Effect are mere correlation of Force, produced by organization or the manner in which forces are concentrated and arranged.

Mr. Grove says, "I use the term force in reference to them (the affections of matter), as meaning the active principle inseparable from matter which is supposed to induce its various changes," † But as "the various changes" are the only things known to us, why assume that they are inseparable from matter, or that there is any matter at all?

* Correlation of Physical Forces, p. 22, by W. R. Grove.
† Ibid, p. 16.

Again, Professor Tyndall says, "We know no more of the origin of force than of the origin of matter; where matter is, force is, for we only know matter through its forces." *

Is it not better then to dispense with matter altogether? For if all action, change, or motion, is owing to force, and it is impossible to conceive of force without antecedent force, what then becomes of matter? This doctrine of the Persistence of Force seems to me, not only to make matter altogether unnecessary, but to exclude even the very idea. I shall use its nomenclature therefore only as signs indicating Force.

Professor John Tyndall says in the eloquent peroration to his work on Heat:—"The discoveries and generalizations of modern science constitute a poem more sublime than has ever yet been addressed to the imagination. The natural philosopher of to-day may dwell amid conceptions which beggar those of Milton. So great and grand are they, that in the contemplation of them *a certain force of character is requisite to preserve us from bewilderment*. Look at the integrated energies of our world—the stored power of our coal-fields, our winds and rivers, our fleets, armies, and guns. What are they? They are all generated by a portion of the sun's energy, which does not amount to one thousand three hundred millionth part of the whole. This is the entire fraction of the sun's force intercepted by the Earth, and we convert but a small fraction of this fraction into mechanical energy. Multiplying all our powers by millions of millions, we do not reach the sun's expenditure. And still, notwithstanding this enormous drain, in the lapse of human history we are unable to detect a diminution of his store. Measured by our largest terrestrial standards, such a reservoir of power is infinite; but it is our privilege to rise above these standards, and to regard

* The Constitution of the Universe.—*Fortnightly Review.*

the sun himself as a speck in infinite extension, a mere drop in the universal sea. We analyze the space in which he is immersed, and which is the vehicle of his power. We pass to other systems and other suns, each pouring forth energy like our own, but still without infringements of the law, which reveals immutability in the midst of change, which recognizes incessant transference, conversion, but neither final gain nor loss. This law generalizes the aphorism of Solomon, that there is nothing new under the sun, by teaching us to detect everywhere, under its infinite variety of appearances, *the same primeval force*. To nature nothing can be added; from nature nothing can be taken away; the sum of her energies is constant, and the utmost man can do in the pursuit of physical truth, or in the application of physical knowledge, is to shift the constituents of the never-varying total. The law of conservation rigidly excludes both creation and annihilation. Waves may change to ripples, and ripples to waves — magnitude may be substituted for number, and number for magnitude — asteroids may aggregate to suns, *suns may resolve themselves into flora, and fauna, and flora and fauna melt in air* — the flux of power is eternally the same, it rolls in music through the ages, and all terrestrial energy — the manifestations of life as well as the display of phenomena — are but modulations."

CHAPTER II.

FORCE; ITS MENTAL CORRELATES.

It is probable that at the origin of our globe, the concentration of force previously diffused in the form of so-called nebulous matter, produced an amount of heat which gradually took the shapes we have now around us. Certain forces were chemically united, as in our primary rocks, others were divorced, as the oxygen from the carbon in the coal. By bringing the carbon and the oxygen in our atmosphere together again we have the same amount of force, in the shape of heat, which it originally took to separate them. It takes an immense amount of force to separate magnesia into oxygen and magnesium, and their reunion is proportionately intense, as is now so beautifully and easily illustrated in the burning of magnesium wire. It is by the action of these forces that most of the changes we see around us are still produced. The force derived from the union of oxygen with the coal annually dug from the British mines is calculated to be equal to that of the whole human race. The light and heat of the sun's rays separated the carbon and oxygen in plants and vegetables, and an immense amount of force is generated whenever the carbon and oxygen again meet, whether it be in the fire-place, or, more amicably and less energetically, in the animal body. Thus Dr. Neil Arnott says:—"James Watt, when devising his great engine, knew well that the rapid combination of the oxygen of atmospheric air with the combustible fuel in the furnace, produced the heat and force of the engine; but he did not know that in living bodies there is going on, only more slowly, a similar combination of the oxygen of the air with the like combustible matter in the food, as this circulates after digestion in the form of blood through the lungs, which combination produces the warmth and force of the living animal. The chief resemblances of the two objects are exhibited strikingly in the following table of comparison, where, in two adjoining columns, are set forth nearly the same things and actions, with difference only in the names:—

The Steam Engine in action takes—	*The animal body in life, takes—*
1. Fuel, viz.: coal and wood, both being old or dry vegetable matter, and both combustible.	1. Food, viz.: recent or fresh vegetable matter and flesh, both being of kindred composition, and both combustible.
2. Water.	2. Drink, (essentially water).
3. Air.	3. Breath, (common air.)
And produces,	*And produces—*
4. Steady boiling heat of 212 degrees by quick combustion.	4. Steady animal heat of 98 degrees, by slow combustion.
5. Smoke from the chimney, or air loaded with carbonic acid and vapour.	5. Foul breath from the windpipe, or air loaded with carbonic acid and vapour.
6. Ashes, part of the fuel which does not burn.	6. Animal refuse, part of the food which does not burn.
7. Motive force, of simple alternate push and pull in the piston, which, acting through levers, joints, bands, &c., does work of endless variety.	7. Motive force, of simple alternate contraction and relaxation in the muscles, which, acting through the levers, joints, tendons, &c., of the limbs, does work of endless variety.

8. A deficiency of fuel, water, or air, first disturbs, and then stops the motion.	8. A deficiency of food, drink, or breath, first disturbs, then stops the motion and the life.
9. Local damage from violence in a machine is repaired by the makers.*	9. Local hurt or disease in a living body is repaired or cured by the action of internal power given by the Creator.

We have here illustrated the mode only in which the force in animals is generated; the form it ultimately takes depends entirely upon the organization through which it has to pass. Life was thought to be a peculiar principle; but it depends for its development and manifestation entirely upon the union of the ordinary physical forces with a peculiar structure or arrangement of forces; for what are called vital forces are only the correlate of physical forces.

In a very small part of the acorn lies the structure that can develop only into an oak, and the human germ, in which lie folded up the wondrous powers of man, is invisible without the aid of the microscope. Life then is only Force acting through special organizations, which organizations, so far as we yet know, are formed only by transmission from parent to offspring; they are always hereditary.

But seeds might remain for ever unchanged — as the wheat in the pyramids, for 8,000 years, until quickened into being by forces from without. "Thus, for example, when a seed is placed in the ground, the first process which takes place within it is one of decomposition. The mass of the seed consists of starch and albumen, in the midst of which is placed a small cellular body, called the germ. This germ will grow, and develop into the future plant, but only on condition that a process of decay goes on in the starchy and albuminous matter with which it is in connection. Part of

* A Survey of Human Progress, p. 159.

the latter sinks into the inorganic state, uniting with oxygen, and passing off as carbonic acid. The young plant is at first of less weight than the seed or root which has disappeared in generating it. When it arrives at the surface of the soil, a new process commences. The rays of the sun, falling on its leaves, maintain in them a continuance of the same process (one of chemical change) by which the first development of the germ was determined. Thus new materials are added to the plant, the light exciting those chemical processes which produce the organic arrangement of fresh portions of matter. The leaves, under the stimulus of the sun's rays, decompose carbonic acid, giving off part of the oxygen, and 'fix,' as it is said, the carbon in union with hydrogen, and sometimes with nitrogen, &c., to form the various vegetable cells and their contents.

"An animal now consumes this plant. In digestion there takes place again a precisely similar process to that with which we started—the germination of the seed. The substance of the plant partially decomposes; a portion of it sinks into a state approximating to the inorganic, while another portion (doubtless by means of the force thus generated) becomes more highly vitalized, and fitted to form part of the animal structure. The germination of the seed, and animal digestion, are parallel processes. Each of them is two-fold—a decomposing and a vitalizing action going on together, the latter having its origin in and depending on the other. Having formed part of the animal structure for a time, this living matter decomposes yet again, and again gives off its force. But now, instead of effecting, as in the previous cases, a vitalizing action, the force produces a mechanical action in the muscles, or a nervous action in the brain, or, in short, the *function* of whatever organ the matter we are tracing may have been incorporated with;—the function being but another mode of operation of the same force which caused the nutrition. And thus, supposing the action to have been a muscular exertion, say the lifting of a weight, we shall have traced the force, which came from the inorganic world at first, in the form of the sun's rays, and was embodied in the substance of the plant, back again into the inorganic world in the form of motion. * * * The plant yields up its life to nourish the animal body, as that body, so nourished, in its activity yields up *its* life to impart force to the world around. * * * Every giving off of force has for its necessary effect the storing up of force in equal amount elsewhere. The two halves of this process cannot be divided." * †

* Physiological Riddles. *Cornhill Magazine.*

† There is an admirable paper on "Vitality", illustrating this subject, in the "Reader" of October 29th, 1864, signed "J. T.", evidently Professor Tyndall. As the subject is of so much importance we make no apology for quoting at some length.

"In what sense, then, is the sun to be regarded as the origin of the energy derivable from plants and animals? Let us try to give an intelligible answer to this question. Water may be raised from the sea-level to a high elevation, and then permitted to descend. In descending it may be made to assume various forms — to fall in cascades, to spurt in fountains, to boil in eddies, or to flow tranquilly along a uniform bed. It may, moreover, be caused to set complex machinery in motion, to turn millstones, throw shuttles, work saws and hammers, and drive piles. But every form of power here indicated would be derived from the original power expended in raising the water to the height from which it fell. There is no energy *generated* by the machinery; the work performed by the water in descending is merely the parcelling out and distribution of the work expended in raising it. In precisely this sense is all the energy of plants and animals the parcelling out and distribution of a power originally exerted by the sun. In the case of the water, the source of the power consists in the forcible separation of a quantity of the liquid from the lowest level of the earth's surface and its elevation to a higher position, the power thus expended being returned by the water in its descent. In the case of vital phenomena, the source of power consists in the forcible separation of the

Thus we see that not a peculiar agent, called Life, but a peculiar mode of operation is required to produce the special results we call vital forces, and as Life is thus the mere correlate of Physical forces, so Mind is the correlate of

---

atoms of chemical compounds by the sun—of the carbon and hydrogen, for example, of the carbonic acid and water diffused throughout the atmosphere, from the oxygen with which they are combined. This separation is effected in the leaves of plants by solar energy. The constituents of the carbonic acid and water are there torn asunder in spite of their mutual attraction, the carbon and hydrogen are stored up in the wood, and the oxygen is set free in the air. When the wood is burned the oxygen recombines with the carbon, and the heat then given out is of the precise amount drawn from the sun to effect the previous "reduction" of the carbonic acid. The reunion of the carbon with the oxygen is similar to the reunion of our falling water with the earth from which it had been separated. We name the one action 'gravity' and the other 'chemical affinity'; but these different names must not mislead us regarding the qualitative identity of the two forces. They are both *attraction*, and, to the intellect, the falling of carbon atoms against oxygen atoms is not more difficult of conception than the falling of water to the earth.

"The building up of the vegetable then is effected by the sun through the reduction of chemical compounds. *All the phenomena of animal life are more or less complicated reversals of these processes of reduction.* We eat the vegetable, and we breathe the oxygen of the air, and in our bodies the oxygen which had been *lifted* from the carbon and hydrogen by the action of the sun again falls towards them, producing animal heat and developing animal forms. Through the most complicated phenomena of vitality this law runs:—the vegetable is produced by the lifting, the animal by the falling of a weight. But the question is not exhausted here. The water which we used in our first illustration produces all the motion displayed in its descent, but the *form* of the motion depends on the character of the machinery interposed in the path of the water. And thus the primary action of the sun's rays is qualified by the atoms and molecules among which their energy is distributed. Molecular forces determine the *form* which the solar energy will assume. In the one case this energy is so conditioned by its atomic machinery as to result in the formation of a cabbage; in another case it is so conditioned as to result in the formation of an oak. So also as

Vital forces. "That no idea or feeling arises, save as a result of some physical force expended in producing it, is fast becoming a common-place of science; and whoever duly weighs the evidence will see, that nothing but an over-

---

regards the reunion of the carbon and the oxygen—the *form* of their reunion is determined by the molecular machinery through which the combining energy acts. In one case the action may result in the formation of a man, while in another it may result in the formation of a grasshopper.

"But whence comes the power on the part of the molecules to compel the solar energy to take determinate forms? The matter of the animal body is that of inorganic nature. There is no substance in the animal tissues which is not primarily derived from the rocks, the water, and the air. Are the forces of organic matter, then, different in kind from those of inorganic matter? All the philosophy of the present day negatives the question. It is the compounding in the organic world of forces that belong equally to the inorganic that constitutes the mystery and the miracle of vitality. Every portion of every animal body may be reduced to purely inorganic matter. A perfect reversal of this process of reduction would carry us from the inorganic to the organic; and such a reversal is at least conceivable. The tendency, indeed, of modern science is to break down the wall of partition between organic and inorganic, and to reduce both to the operation of forces which are the same in kind, but whose combinations differ in complexity.

"The mode in which these combinations have been brought about is a perfectly legitimate subject of scientific speculation; and in this we will here so far indulge as to ask a single speculative question. It is generally supposed that our earth once belonged to the sun, from which it was detached in a molten condition. Hence arises the question 'Did that incandescent world contain latent within itself the elements of life?' Or, supposing a planet carved from our present sun, and set spinning round him at the distance of our earth, would one of the consequences of its refrigeration be the development of organic forms? *Structural* forces certainly lie latent in the molten mass, whether or not those forces reach to the extent of forming a plant or an animal. All the marvels of crystalline force, all those wonderful branching frost-ferns which cover our window-panes on a winter morning—the exquisite molecular architecture which is now known to belong to the ice of our frozen lakes—all this 'constructiveness' lies latent in an amorphous

whelming bias in favour of a pre-conceived theory, can explain its non-acceptance. How this metamorphosis takes place—how a force existing as emotion, heat, or light, can become a mode of consciousness—how it is possible for aerial vibrations to generate the sensation we call sound, or for the forces liberated by chemical changes in the brain to give rise to motion—these are mysteries which it is impossible to fathom. But they are not profounder mysteries than the transformation of the physical forces into each other. They are not more completely beyond our comprehension than the natures of Mind and Matter. They have simply the same insolubility as all other ultimate questions. We can learn nothing more than that here is one of the uniformities in the order of phenomena."*

The peculiar mode of operation which force assumes, whether as mechanical force or motion, heat, magnetism, or feeling, emotion, or thought, depends, as we have said, upon organization or structure, that is, upon the arrangement of

---

drop of water, and comes into play when the water is sufficiently cooled. And who will set limits to the possible play of molecular forces in the cooling of a planet?

"In discussing these questions it is impossible to avoid taking side-glances at the phenomena of intellect and will. Are they, by natural evolution, capable of being developed from incandescent matter? Whether they are or not, we do not seem to possess the rudiments of an organ which could enable us to comprehend the change; we are utterly incompetent to take the step from the phenomena of physics to those of consciousness. And, even granting the validity of the above explanation, the questions still remain, 'Who or what made the sun and gave his rays such power? Who or what bestowed upon the ultimate particles of matter the forces whose interaction, combined with the energy of the solar rays, produces plants and animals?' Science does not know: the mystery, though pushed back, remains as deep as ever."

* First Principles, by *Herbert Spencer*, p. 280.

PECULIARITIES OF STRUCTURE. 15

permanent centres of force. The Natural Philosopher is constantly coming near to this fact, without seeing its full significance. Thus Liebig says, "Isomorphism, or the quality of form of many chemical compounds having a different composition, tends to prove that matter consists of atoms, the mere *arrangement* of which produces all the properties of bodies. But when we find that a *different arrangement* of the *same* elements gives rise to various physical and chemical properties, and a *similar arrangement* of *different* elements produces properties very much the same, may we not inquire whether some of those bodies which we regard as elements, may not be merely modifications of the same substance, whether they are not the same matter in different states of arrangement?" * All we have to consider is Force as it passes through the living structure of the human body, in its various modes of operation.

The peculiarities of structure which modify the form and action of force in the human body depend principally upon the stock, or race, from which the individual is descended. Among animals almost any form and quality of the species can be produced by crossing, but whether these changes can be said to be improvements upon the original type is another thing. Certainly mongrels among dogs and horses are not considered to be any improvement, and the same may almost invariably be said of mixed races of men; the higher type loses what the inferior gains. The mixing of English and Hindoo blood often results in feebleness of brain bordering on fatuity or insanity. The modern Mexican — a mixture of the Spaniard and the native Indian, is an inferior race, &c. We are familiar with this influence of stock in what is called budding and grafting in trees. A bud of one tree introduced into the

* Chemical Lectures, p. 54.

bark of another retains all the peculiarities of its original
parentage, and a small branch of one tree transferred to
another retains all the specialities that distinguish its fruit,
although dependent entirely upon the root, stock, and circu-
latory system of another tree. Although we can trace no
difference of structure between the graft and the branch to
which it is attached, no doubt it is there that the difference
lies, it is upon that difference of arrangement that the
modification of the vital force depends. That the new branch
should retain all the specialities of its parent stock under
such circumstances is both wonderful and instructive, for
the same kind of budding and grafting is constantly going
on in the intermarriages of human beings, although the
fruit individuals bear in consequence passes almost unnoticed.
There are certain broadly-marked constitutional qualities,
however, which have not escaped notice. These have been
called by Phrenologists the Temperaments. "There are four
temperaments," we are told by Mr. George Combe, "accompanied by different degrees of strength and activity in the
brain — the *lymphatic*, the *sanguine*, the *bilious*, and the
nervous. The temperaments are supposed to depend upon
the constitution of particular systems of the body: the brain
and nerves being predominantly active from constitutional
causes, seem to produce the nervous temperament; the lungs,
heart, and blood-vessels being constitutionally predominant,
to give rise to the sanguine; the muscular and fibrous system to the bilious; and the glands and assimilating organs
to the lymphatic." * These differences and their combinations are very obviously marked and indicate great differences
in the bodily and mental characters of individuals. There is
a very wide field, however, open for observation beyond; the

* System of Phrenology, p. 50.

bilious or fibrous temperament, for instance, is said to give endurance, but it is by no means sufficient to account for the great power of endurance of bodily fatigue that distinguished such men as Napoleon Buonaparte; the nervous temperament is supposed to give great mental activity, but this does not account for the kind of memory said to be possessed by Sir Walter Scott and others, by which they were enabled to remember almost all they read. These and many similar powers probably depend upon some peculiar quality or structure of body and brain yet unobserved.

The Brain is the organ of mind, that is, it is in the brain and nervous system that the correlation or change of force takes place which distinguishes thought and feeling from heat, electricity, magnetism, &c., and we have the equivalent of that force again in muscular action, heat, electricity, &c.

The brain has a peculiar structure fitting it for its peculiar electrical and galvanic operations; thus, Professor Ehrenberg asserts that by means of the microscope he has discovered the fibres of the encephalon, spinal chord, and nerves, to be tubular, i. e., that they do not consist of solid fibres, but of parallel or fasciculated tubes, dilated at intervals or jointed, and from one-ninety-sixth to one-three-thousandth parts of a line in diameter. Also, that they contain a perfectly transparent tenacious fluid, never visibly globular, the *liquor nerveus*, which differs from the nervous medulla as the chyle does from blood. * †

---

* Human Physiology, p. 466. *Dr. Elliotson.*
† To what extent the more recent researches of Dr. Lionel Beale, as given in his paper on "the Paths of Nerve-currents", in the Proceedings of the Royal Society, vol. xiii., p. 386, confirm those of Ehrenberg, I am not able to say,—as I have not the book at hand. But Mr. Bain tells us that "for every fibre coming up from the senses, and every fibre going out to the limbs and moving organs there must

The dependance of the mind upon the bodily organization, and upon the force derived from the food acting through it, now needs no proof. The mind like the body has its several ages—it is childish in childhood, strong in manhood, weak in sickness, frenzied in madness, and doting in old age. It sympathises with digestion, and changes with each change in the blood. If the circulation is rapid it quickens thought, so that in fever we have delirium, and from excess of alcohol delirium tremens. With excess of carbonic acid the action ceases altogether, and with excess of oxygen (nitrous oxygen or laughing gas) the action is greatly increased. If the purifying organs are out of order we have serious mental depression, and if we abstract heat or give chloroform, first mental action and then vitality ceases altogether; but mental action first.

The dependance of the thinking power upon the food requires no proof, as thinking ceases altogether if food is too long withheld; but close observation shows that not only do alcohol, opium, and hashish * act upon the mind in the mode

---

be at least 10,000, perhaps 100,000 traversing the brain, involving a great and rapid multiplication in the progress through the cerebral substance.—*The Fortnightly Review*, January, 1866.

* Besides the various effects which are common to all the principal narcotics, each has characteristics of its own. Hashish produces real catalepsy, and exaggerates rather than prevents the report of the external senses as to external objects; the thorn-apple, on the other hand, causes truly spectral illusions, and enables the Indian to converse with the spirit of his ancestors. The Siberian fungus gives insensibility to pain without interfering with consciousness. The common buff-ball stops all muscular action, and leaves the perceptive powers untouched. Coccoins Indious makes the body drunk, without affecting the mind. Coca has the wonderful power of sustaining muscular strength in the absence of food, and of preventing the wasting of the tissues of the body during the greatest and most prolonged exertion. The effects of the

with which we are familiar, but all kinds of food affect the mind differently, causing difference in action. But if the food acts upon the mind, so does the mind upon the food; "When the pneumo-gastric or chief nerve of the stomach is tied or cut through, and its end separated so as to interrupt the flow of nervous energy towards that organ, digestion is either entirely arrested or greatly impaired.*

But the brain and nervous system dominate in all parts of the system, and influence both its action and form. The brain is nourished by the heart, and if it ceased for one instant to send its blood to the brain, Sensibility would cease; and the heart equally depends for motive power upon the brain. "Powerful mental shocks momently arrest the heart, and sometimes arrest it for ever. That which a powerful current will do applied to a pneumogastric nerve, will be done by a profound agitation of grief or joy— truly called a heart-shaking influence. The agitation of the great centres of thought is communicated to the spinal chord, and from it to the nerves which issue to different parts of the body; the limbs are violently moved, the glands are excited to increased activity, the tears flow, the facial muscles contract, the chest expands, laughter or sobs, dances of delight and shouts of joy, these and the manifold expressions of an agitated emotion are the after results— the first effect is an arrest, more or less fugitive, followed

---

different narcotics are not only peculiar, but often opposed. Opium and Hashish, common in most of their effects, are opposite in this, that the former diminishes sensibility to external impressions, whereas the latter almost infinitely increases it. Betel is even an antidote to opium, as tea is to alcohol. Tobacco suspends mental activity; opium and hashish increase it a thousand fold.—*National Review*, p. 91, Jan., 1858.

* Dr. A. Combe on Digestion and Dietetics, p. 77.

by an increase of the heart's action. If the organism be vigorous, the effect of a powerful emotion is a sudden paleness, indicating a momentary arrest of the heart. This may be but for an instant: the heart pauses, and the lungs pause with it—'the breath is taken away.' This is succeeded by an energetic palpitation; the lungs expand, the blood rushes to the face and brain with increased force. Should the organism be sickly or highly sensitive, the arrest is of longer duration, and fainting, more or less prolonged, is the result. In a very sensitive or very sickly organization the arrest is final. The shock of joy and the shock of grief have both been known to kill."*

The Brain and Nervous System influence not only the functions, but the growth of the whole body, regulating the form both of the muscles and bones—of expression and action, and thus physiognomy and chirognomy are legitimate sciences.†

But it is a limited quantity of force that is derived from the food, and the mode of its action depends upon its distribution over the body, and the functions it has there to perform. This is regulated, as we have seen, greatly by the Temperaments. While digestion is going on the powers of thinking and feeling are proportionately decreased; so also great bodily exercise and great mental activity are incompatible. Again, the great activity of one portion of the brain decreases the energy of another—a predominating intellect weakens feeling, and an active propensity the moral sentiments. This distribution of force explains many hitherto

* The Heart and the Brain, by G. H. Lewes.—*The Fortnightly Review.*
† See Psychonomy of the Hand, according to MM. D'Arpentigny and Desbarrolles, by Richard Beamish, F.R.S. London, F. Pitman, 20, Paternoster Row.

mysterious physiological phenomena. In the nomad tribes and the agricultural population, where great muscular outdoor exercise is required, and the vital system consequently greatly predominates, the vis medicatrix, or natural healing power, is much stronger than in people of sedentary and studious habits, and the one class recovers from accidents that would be death to the other. So also studious habits or strong feelings impair vital power. The sexual feeling is generally the strongest in the system and absorbs the largest amount of force, and when it comes into too early activity, it stops the growth of the body, and a large amativeness is generally attended with deficient locomotive or muscular power. The emasculated London cats grow to greater size than their unmutilated brethren in the country, and geldings and oxen have much more working power, that is, enduring muscular force, than stallions and bulls. When the important vital action,—the renovation of the body by putting in new tissue, is going on, the action of the Mind ceases altogether, and what we call sleep—more or less perfect, supervenes.

But the Brain, as the organ of Mind, is not a single organ, but a congeries or bundle of organs, manifesting a plurality of faculties, with force in proportion to the size and quality of the organ.

Mind as a force, as a function or power of Brain, should be studied as other forces, in its manifestations—in its attributes—by what it does.

Examined in this way, Dr. Gall discovered that a strong verbal memory was always accompanied by a prominent eye, which prominence he found to depend upon the large size of a convolution of the brain, lying at the back of the eye. Pursuing his investigations he found that the special talents of the musician, the sculptor, the artist, the mathematician, the calculator, the metaphysician, &c., were dependent upon different parts of the brain, and he and his followers, after long and repeated observation, have come to the knowledge of what faculties and feelings and what parts of the brain are mutually connected.

As all organizations differ, and that which is true of one mind, therefore, can only be relatively true of another, reflection upon the consciousness which such organization supplies, cannot alone be the true method of investigating mind, it can be pursued only in conjunction with external observation.

Following this method Phrenologists have established the following chart of our Intellectual Faculties:—

INTELLECTUAL FACULTIES, *which perceive existence.*
Individuality—Takes cognizance of existence and simple facts.
Form—Renders men observant of Form.
Size—Renders men observant of dimensions, and aids perspective.
Weight—Communicates the perception of momentum, weight, resistance, and aids equilibrium.
Colouring—Gives perception of colour.

INTELLECTUAL FACULTIES, *which perceive the relations of external objects.*
Locality—Gives the idea of space and relative position.
Number—Gives the talent for calculation.
Order—Communicates the love of physical arrangement.
Eventuality—Takes cognizance of occurrences and events.
Time—Gives rise to the perception of duration.
Tune—The sense of melody arises from it.
Language—Gives a facility in acquiring a knowledge of arbitrary signs to express thoughts—readiness in the use of them; and a power of inventing them.

REFLECTIVE FACULTIES, *which compare, judge, and discriminate.*
Comparison—Gives the power of discovering analogies, resemblances, and differences.

Causality—Traces the dependencies of phenomena, and the relations of cause and effect.

The External Senses of Feeling or Touch, Taste, Smell, Hearing, and Sight, are necessary to connect these faculties with the external world, and to bring them into activity.

The above phrenological organs furnish what are called by metaphysicians the *à priori* forms of thought. The raw force, if I may use the expression, taken in with the food at one part of the machine, is by the action of external force upon these organs, manufactured into the beautiful phantasmagoria of the external world.

SECTION I.

THE PSYCHOLOGY OF PHRENOLOGY.

> "We are such stuff,
> As dreams are made of, and our little life
> Is rounded by a sleep."—*Shakspeare.*

> "*Omne quod cognoscitur non secundum sui vim, sed secundum cognoscentium potius comprehenditur facultatem.*"—"All that is known is comprehended, not according to its own force, but according rather to the faculty of those knowing."—*Boethius.*

> "For man's sense is falsely asserted to be the standard of things. On the contrary all the perceptions, both of the sense and of the mind, have reference to Man, and not to the universe."—*Bacon, Nov. Org., Aph. 41.*

By careful observation of the action of the primitive faculties we are able to determine most of those psychological questions upon which metaphysical philosophers are still disputing, as Mill on Hamilton, Herbert Spencer on Mill, &c.

The facts observed by the cerebral physiologists or phrenologists, however at present ignored and repudiated, furnish the test of the truth of these various conflicting systems. The Intellectual Faculties supply us with ideas, which ideas are only slight feelings or sensations, differing from our other feelings only in intensity.

A perception of ideas and feelings pass through the mind, or rather constitute the mind; upon this succession we reflect or are conscious, and the only objects of knowledge are these ideas and feelings. We are conscious of nothing but these changes, and we never really advance one step beyond ourselves, or can *know* any kind of existence but those perceptions that lie in that narrow compass.

We *infer*, however, that these ideas are connected with the brain, that the brain is in connection with the senses, and that the senses are acted upon by something external.

But it is ideas only of which we are conscious, and it is these only therefore we can be said to know; of this "something external" we know nothing, and by what name we call it therefore signifies little. Matter and Force are the names we give to this non-ego. The properties of matter which are supposed to distinguish it from force, are, as we shall see, mere forms of thought, "clusters of sensations"; correlated force.

The combination of forces which compose our own bodies, certain centres or reservoirs of which constitute the reality of the external world, clearly exist independently of perception, and are not mere abstractions, and if we disconnect the percipient from these external forces perception ceases. The organs of the Brain, through which the correlation of vital force to mental takes place, are of two kinds; those which are acted upon by external causes, through the medium of the senses, and the ideas belonging to which, therefore are modified by the sense; and those faculties which act upon these ideas when so furnished by the first class. They have been divided into ideas of Simple and Relative Perception.

All the knowledge we have therefore of an external world is of its action through the medium of the senses upon only a few of the mental faculties, and which perceptive faculties alone would be quite insufficient to give us the idea of nature as we now conceive of it. The world, as it appears to us — as it exists in the region of our consciousness, is created in our own minds by the action of the faculties of Relative Perception and of Reflection upon the comparatively few ideas furnished by the faculties of Simple Perception.

Our ideas of things result from the relation between the object or cause, the sense, and the three classes of intellectual faculties; and the vain effort to untie this untieable synthesis has caused most of the errors of the metaphysician.

"What we term the properties of an object, are the powers it exerts of producing sensations in our consciousness."* The object acts upon the sense, and the sense upon the perceptive faculties of Form, Size, Weight, Colour, &c., and we have ideas of shapes and sizes and colours, of extension, of weight, of solidity, hardness, strength, &c., and these we call the properties of matter. The idea of extension and solidity, which is supposed peculiarly to distinguish matter, is derived from the faculties of form, size, and colour, which give the shape, and weight, the sense of resistance. Individuality unites these qualities into one, and gives the idea of the individual or substratum or noumenon upon which they are supposed to depend. "The name 'rose' is the mark of the sensation of colour, a sensation of shape, a sensation of touch, a sensation of smell, all in conjunction

* J. S. Mill.

(an action of the senses and intellectual faculties combined). * * * Of those names (such as rose) which denote clusters of sensation, it is obvious that some include a greater some a less, number of sensations. * * * We not only give names to clusters of sensations, but to clusters of clusters, that is to a number of minor clusters united into a greater cluster. Thus we give the name 'wood' to a particular cluster of sensations, the name canvas to another, the name rope to another. To these clusters and many others, joined together in one great cluster, we give the name ship. * * * And again, in using the names tree, horse, man, the names of what I call objects, I am referring only to my own sensations (and to other people's sensations); in fact, therefore, only naming a certain number of sensations, regarded as in a particular state of combination; that is, in concomitance." * Accordingly, we name only our own sensation or idea, but this idea is compounded equally of the object, the sense, and the intellectual faculties, each of which we know can exist separately. Thus the noise which we say we hear in the street, is a sensation really in our own head, although the cause of the sensation is in the street and each has a separate and distinct existence. The cause in the street may affect other people in the same way, and have numberless other effects, while the sensation is a correlate of physical forces, proceeding from or put in motion in the street, which may again become physical force and take its place in the external world. The ego and the non-ego thus pass and repass into each other and are constantly changing places.

INDIVIDUALITY.—It is the form of thought peculiar to the organ of Individuality that gives oneness or unity to

* *James Mill.*

these clusters of sensations. We individualize all our own parts and functions, and call it our body; we do the same with reference to the succession of our ideas, and call it our mind.

IDENTITY.—The feeling of Personal Identity which we attach to this evanescent "cluster of ideas" which we call body and mind, results from a primitive mental faculty, or instinct, connected with its special organ in the brain. This is evidenced by the organ sometimes becoming diseased, when the feeling of Identity—the "I" of consciousness, becomes lost, or double, or otherwise deranged.

BELIEF.—Each intellectual faculty and feeling supplies us with an instinct or intuition, and it is in the action of these faculties, in the intuitions supplied by them, that mankind necessarily believe. They furnish our fundamental truths. Faith or belief is not an action of the intellectual faculties, but a sentiment or feeling, and it is as easy to believe in one order of nature, or set of sequences, as in another, until experience or the intellect has determined what are permanent or invariable. Of course we can believe only in what we understand; when we are said to believe in the incomprehensible, we believe only in the testimony, or in so much only as we do understand.

CONSCIOUSNESS, AND ITS RELIABILITY.—And now comes the question: are our Instincts or Intuitions worthy of belief? These intuitions, resulting from the action of our primitive faculties, constitute our Consciousness;—is the verdict of consciousness to be accepted without appeal, or can we reject its testimony? First, we must examine what is consciousness, and what is the nature of its verdict. James Mill says, "To have a feeling is to be conscious; and to be conscious is to have a feeling;" and J. S. Mill says, "To feel and not to know that we feel is an impossibility." Now the brutes have feelings, but there is no evidence that they are conscious of them; they feel, but do not know that they feel. They have consciousness, but are not conscious; for consciousness is used by most writers to mean sensibility or feeling; but to be conscious is to reflect on this sensibility or feeling. The brute when it chews the cud has a succession of slightly pleasurable feelings, the aggregate of which constitute a mild kind of happiness. It cannot be said to be conscious of this, but there is not less happiness because it does not reflect upon it. The faculties by which we know and feel, and those by which we know that we know and feel, are different, and one class—the reflective faculties—judges of the trustworthiness of the other. But there is no more a distinct act of consciousness attending every act of mind, than there is a distinct act of Will attending every act of body. Nature consists of "what perceives and what is perceived," but this is merely one class of mental faculty acting upon another—that is, reflection on consciousness. "What we perceive under the condition of contact or touch, say the Berkelians, are sensations only, and not the causes of sensations." Now the cause is certainly contained in the sensation perceived, which is the resultant equally of the cause or object, the sense, and the mental faculty, that is, the sensation is the correlate or exact equivalent of the force without and the nervous force within.

BELIEF IN AN EXTERNAL WORLD.—The generality of mankind believe in an External World as it appears to them, as something without and entirely independent of themselves; they know nothing of consciousness and of sensations. They understand nothing and believe nothing about the "objects of knowledge being ideas," they believe only in things which are hot or cold, rough or smooth, hard or soft, coloured, &c. They have "an instantaneous and irresistible conviction of outward objects," but they know nothing of "Permanent Possibilities of Sensation." They believe in material objects, and not in modifications of our sensibility, or the Relativity of our Knowledge. It is the non-ego, and not the mind perceiving, in which we first believe, and this conviction is not slowly acquired, but is instinctive or intuitional—the result of our primitive faculties.* It is doubt

* "What do mankind in general believe? They believe that the material world is exactly and in every respect the world which our senses report to us as external to ourselves. They believe that the rocks, the hills, the trees, the stars, that we all see, are not mere hieroglyphics of a something different from themselves and from us, but are really what is there. That outer vastness of space in which orbs are shining and wheeling is no mere representation or visionary allegory of something; it is the thing itself. This is, and always has been, the popular belief of mankind in general. All mankind may therefore be described, generally, as Natural Realists. But, strange to say, Natural Realism has been the system of but one or two modern philosophers—among whom Reid is named as a type. Nay, more, among these philosophers it is not the popular form of the belief that is entertained. Mankind in general suppose sweetness, shrillness, colour, &c., to be qualities inherently belonging to the objects to which they are attributed, while the philosophers who are Natural Realists admit that at least these so-called 'secondary qualities' of objects have no proper oneness, but are only physiological affections,—affections of the organs of taste, hearing, sight, &c., produced by particular objects. Thus the Natural Realism of philosophers is itself a considerable remove from the Natural Realism of the crude popular belief. It does not, with the crude popular belief, call the whole apparent world, of sights, sounds, tastes, tacts, and odours the real world that would be there whether man were there or not; true, it descries in that apparent world a block or core, if I may so say, which would have to be thought of as really existing, even if there were swept away all that consists in our rich physiological interactions with it.

"According to this system (Constructive Idealism) we do not perceive the real external world immediately, but only mediately—that is, the objects which we take as the things actually perceived are not the real objects at all, but only vicarious assurances, representatives, or nuncii of real unknown objects. The hills, the rocks, the trees, the stars, all the choir of heaven and earth, are not, in any of their qualities, primary,

that is acquired, and we ask ourselves, Are these intuitions to be relied on? For as Fichte says, speaking of a tree and things external, "there is in fact nothing there, but only a manifestation of Power from something that is not I." Kant also observes "that there is an illusion inherent in our constitutions; that we cannot help conceiving as belonging to Things themselves, attributes with which they are only clothed by the laws of our sensitive and intellectual nature." To affirm so much, however, is not to reject the testimony of consciousness; for when one class of faculties—the reasoning faculties, tests the testimony of another class, any resulting contradiction is the testimony of consciousness.

"The action of the intellectual faculties in imparting knowledge, is much more simple in its character than the infinite variety of ideas would at first induce us to sup-

---

secondary, or whatever we choose to call them, the actual existence out of us, but only the addresses of a 'something', to our physiology, or adductions by our physiology out of a 'something.' They are all Thoughts or Ideas, with only this peculiarity involved in them, that they will not rest in themselves, but compel a reference to objects out of self, with which, by some arrangement or other, they stand in relation. Difficult as this system may be to understand, and violently as it wrenches the popular common sense, it is yet the system into which the great majority of philosophers in all ages and countries hitherto are seen, more or less distinctly, to have been carried by their speculations. While the Natural Realists among philosophers have been very few, and even these have been Realists in a sense unintelligible to the popular mind, quite a host of philosophers have been Constructive Idealists. These might be further subdivided according to particular variations in the form of their Idealism. Thus, there have been many Constructive Idealists who have regarded the objects rising to the mind in external perception, and taken to be representative of real unknown objects, as something more than modifications of the mind itself—as having their origin without. Among these have been reckoned Mallebranche, Berkeley, Clarke, Sir Isaac Newton, Tucker, and possibly Locke."—Recent British Philosophy, p. 68, et seq. *Professor Masson.*

pose. Thus we perceive qualities of form, size, colour, &c., and we attach these qualities to individual existences: we perceive the number, arrangement and relative position of such existences, and conceive of them as existing in *space;* we have ideas also of motion and active phenomena, and conceive of their existence in *time:* we trace also resemblances and differences, and relations of antecedence and consequence, and distinguish between invariable antecedents called -causes, and such as are not permanent. Now some of the faculties that produce this mental action have direct relation to external objects, and others have relation only to the ideas furnished by them; so that part of our ideas only being furnished by external causes, and part by the action of the mental faculties upon these ideas, we cannot say that all our knowledge comes through the senses. Certain impressions received from without are by the mind itself worked up into a picture which we suppose to belong, or to have its prototype, in the external world, but which is, in fact, manufactured in the mind, and exists only in minds similarly constituted." *

Now what say our Reasoning powers of a world thus created? Contrary to the impressions supplied by Individuality, they tell us that there are no such things as individuals.† We find a world of effects, no causes—a succession of persistent forces:—

> "Nothing in this world is single,
> All things by a law divine
> In one another's being mingle."

The solidified gases which constitute man's bodily indivi-

---

* Philosophy of Necessity. p. 192.

† As we have said, every correlation or change of force creates a new existence or individuality, but it is part only of the great whole, and could have no existence separately.

duality are in constant flux and change with all around,—
and his mind is a succession of separate correlated forces or
ideas. As Hume says, " 'Tis still true, that every distinct
perception, which enters into the composition of the mind,
is a distinct existence, and is different, and distinguishable,
and separable from every other perception, either contemporary or successive." If there be any individuality here, it
belongs to every separate thought; but this individuality is
absorbed, as we shall find, in the One Substance, the only
Unity.

EXTENSION AND SPACE.—But the external world is supposed to be extended; but what is Extension? It results from
the joint action of the organs of Form, Size, and Weight, that
is, it is a compound idea. As Hume says, "The very idea
of extension is copied from nothing but an impression, and
consequently must perfectly agree to it." But he also says,
" Can any one conceive a passion of a yard in length, a foot
in breadth, and an inch in thickness? Thought therefore
and extension are qualities wholly incompatible, and never
can incorporate together into one subject." The same must
be said of Space, so far as the idea of it is based upon
Extension. But is not our idea of Space derived from the
existence of other beings, of things without ourselves whose
nature or essence is thought and force? The idea of extension
is excluded from thought and force. The ego and non-ego
must occupy different positions, and it is this that gives us
the idea of Space. It is the form of thought furnished by
the organ of locality, joined, perhaps, to the idea of extension.

THE DISTINCTION BETWEEN PRIMARY AND SECONDARY
QUALITIES NOT TENABLE.—The distinction which metaphysicians make between the Primary and Secondary Qualities
of bodies is untenable; the external cause of colour is equally
existent with those which give the ideas of solidity and

extension, and equally existent whether the percipient be present or not. Mr. J. S. Mill, however, says, "The sensations answering to the Secondary Qualities are only occasional, those to the Primary, constant. The Secondary, moreover, vary with different persons, and with the primary sensibility of our organs: the Primary, when perceived at all, are, as far as we know, the same to all persons and at all times." Now the fact is, that the strength of these perceptions is exactly in proportion to the size of the organs with which they are connected. People are met with who cannot distinguish one colour from another, and others are equally blind as to forms and sizes, and who could no more be taught to draw than a person with a small organ of colour could paint, or one with a deficient organ of Tune could be taught music. Mr. Mill, however, elsewhere says truly, "How do we know that magnitude is not exclusively a property of our sensations—of the states of subjective consciousness which objects produce in us? (It certainly is quite as much so as colour.) Or, he continues, if this supposition displeases, how do we know that magnitude is not, as Kant considered it, a form of our minds, an attribute with which the laws of thought invest every conception that we can form, but to which there may be something analagous in the Noumenon, the Thing in itself?" Kant's *categories* are his mode of arriving by Reflection on consciousness at the list of Intellectual Faculties or modes of thought which Gall and his followers have arrived at by observation, and they correspond, more correctly than in any other system, to the faculties of Simple and Relative Perception and Reasoning Powers. Our ideas of Relative Perception are not derived from experience; they are innate ideas or intuitions not derived from without, and have therefore no objective reality. These faculties act upon those which perceive existence, give to their modes of thought symmetry and order; each adds its part, the peculiar form it is its province to create, and the picture is painted in our consciousness, which we call the external world.

RELATIVITY OF OUR KNOWLEDGE.—We know then only how we are affected by things external; we know only the world which such affections create in us; what effect the same causes may have acting on other beings, differently constituted, it is impossible to say, neither can we tell what worlds so created lie *without* the sphere of our consciousness,—and we cannot be too modest in our ignorance.

THE WILL.—The Will is the *trigger* of the mind. Upon the "last dictate of the understanding" it lets off the accumulated mental force in the direction of the object or purpose aimed at. The strength of the Will is in proportion to the force to be discharged, which force depends upon the size and quality of the organs of the brain in which the determination originates. The Will has an organ of its own, lying, according to Mr. Atkinson, behind the "Ego" or "I" of consciousness and close to Firmness; thus we get its characteristic expression "I will", and its excess or abuse "wilfulness", and when joined to large Firmness it is determined or persistent Will. When Combativeness governs the Will, the force is generally discharged outwardly; when Cautiousness or Secretiveness prevail, inwardly; often then disturbing the balance of other vital and mental forces. The Will no more lets off itself than the trigger of a gun does: it is generally pulled by the stronger motive, as understanding or mere feeling may prevail.

SECTION II.

THE PERSISTENCE OF FORCE.

"Human Liberty of which all boast, consists solely in this, that man is conscious of his will, and unconscious of the causes by which it is determined."—*Spinoza.*

But if the generality of mankind have deceived themselves in believing in the real existence of an external world as it appears to them, and their intellectual faith is untenable, so is their moral belief equally unsound and fallacious. They believe in Free Will, that is in the power of originating volitions—of an absolute commencement of action in themselves—whereas in nature there is no beginning, merely pre-existent and persistent force and its correlates. All tendencies, all volition and action, are manifestations of effects. "For each manifestation of force can be interpreted only as the effect of some antecedent force: no matter whether it be an inorganic action, an animal movement, a thought or feeling."—First Principles, by *Herbert Spencer.* We know nothing of cause but as the immediate antecedent in the great chain of events going back to eternity, and centring in the One only originating and efficient cause of all things. It is easy to see how this error on the Freedom of the Will originates. The Will, is governed by the last dictate of the understanding, or of our impelling instincts—our propensities and sentiments; and we are conscious that our volitions originate in ourselves. By ourselves we mean the aggregate of all our mental powers. Now we are conscious of the action of our mental powers, but not of the external forces in which they originate and upon which they depend; hence arises the delusion.* Again, we believe we are free because we can do as we please, but what we please to do depends upon our natural powers, which of course are derived, as we did not endow ourselves with them.†

* "It is true that, in common language, the will is spoken of as the first cause of conscious thoughts and acts, but no act of will (that is, of mental energising) can occur without its necessary co-existents and antecedents—that is, its causes; and such as these are, so will the act of will be. There is, in fact, no more a spontaneous act of will than there is spontaneous generation. Strictly such an act is a creation and belongs only to creative power."—Mind and Brain, p. 275. *Dr. Laycock*.

† The *Spectator* in an article on Science and Miracle, January 27, 1866, says, "It is probably true indeed that in some sense the physical forces of the Universe are an invariable quantity, which only alter their forms and not their sum total. If I move my arm, the motion, says the physiologist, is only the exact equivalent of a certain amount of heat which has disappeared and taken the form of that motion. If I do not move it, the heat remains for use in some other way. In either case the stock of force is unchanged. This is the conviction of almost all scientific men and is probably true. But whether the stock of physical force is constant or not, the certainty that human will can change its direction and application—can transfer it from one channel to another—is just the same. And what that really means, if Will be ever free and uncaused, though of course not unconditioned,—which is, we take it, as ultimate and *scientific* a certainty as any in the Universe,—is no less than this,—that a strictly supernatural power alters the order and constitution of nature,—takes a stock of physical force lying in a reservoir here and transfers it to a stream of effort there,—in short, that the supernatural can change the order and constitution of the natural,—in its essence *pure miracle*, though miracle of human, and not of divine origin." When the writer says that the Will is free but not "unconditioned" we might suppose that he means what we do,— that we can all do as we please *subject* to the laws of our own being and the circumstances in which we are placed; but how that can be "conditioned" and yet "uncaused" it is difficult to say. Sir William Hamilton who invented the word, says (Discussions, p. 6,) he means by Conditioned, *determined thought*. How can that be uncaused then, or "free", which is "determined"? How this is to be reconciled we are told by Sir William Hamilton when he comes to explain the Philosophy of the

ETHICS ON A FALSE BASE. 87

Upon this assumed Freedom a whole system of error and superstition has been raised, but it is time now that Ethics were put upon the same footing as all other departments of science. The airs that man has given himself, and his assumption of superiority over all his brethren of the sentient

---

Conditioned "Things there are, he tells us (Discussions, p. 624,) which may, nay must, be true, of which the understanding is wholly unable to construe to itself the possibility." "The Conditioned is the mean between the two extremes—two unconditionates, exclusive of each other, neither of which can be conceded as possible, but of which, on the principles of contradiction and excluded middle, one must be admitted as necessary." (Ibid. p. 15.) Of the two irreconcileable propositions—Necessity and Free Will, the exigencies of the Spectator's creed require that he should accept the latter, although "his understanding may be wholly unable to construe to itself the possibility." The principles of all men of Science equally require that they should accept the former. How, therefore, the Spectator can assume that half the phenomena in the Universe—those dependent on Volition or Will, are uncaused, is a scientific certainty, it is difficult to say. Science, on the contrary, determines that every effect has a cause,—an invariable antecedent, which is always equal, in the same circumstances, to produce the same effect. But an effect without a cause is to produce something from nothing, and this is constantly being repeated in every act of volition; a fact of which the "understanding is wholly unable to construe to itself the possibility," but it is the more to be believed by a Hamiltonian I suppose in consequence. It would indeed be a miracle, as the Spectator affirms! The power of cause, we are told, that "changes the order and constitution of the natural" is super-natural, but that which determines this power to act is nothing, or *no cause!* To say that the Will determines *itself* is no way of escape from the difficulty, as there must be a cause why it determines to act in one way rather than in another. In fact a free will is an absurdity, if not an impossibility, for as long as it remains free, that is, undetermined by some motive or cause, it must be perfectly passive and useless or rather *no will at all*, but merely a conflicting state of mind:—the mind may deliberate, but while it deliberates there is no will. How can a man will that about which he is undecided or uncertain—and when will is thus determined and prepared for action how can it be free? If free it is not will, if

creation are a little ridiculous viewed in this light of the persistence of force.

As we are obliged to admit the Relativity of our Knowledge, and we *know things* only as they affect us intellectually, so, morally, we judge of *actions* only as they affect us. As, however, all actions are the necessary result of pre-existent force, they are all morally alike *in themselves*—right and

---

determined it is not *free*. "Assurance only breeds resolve." But free with most libertarians, means self-determined, not uncaused, as with the *Spectator*, but *self* in this case, means all the attributes and powers we have derived from Nature and the action upon them of the then existing circumstances. I am not surprised that "free will" has been consigned to the region of the supernatural, for there is nothing free in nature, all there is determined according to calculable law. It is not very long since the most ordinary physical effects—the causes not being evident or understood—were supposed to be supernatural and each nation had its own peculiar way of propitiating the unknown Agent: now, in civilised countries, the supernatural is retained only in the department of mind, where the same ignorance exists as formerly in physics, and people try to avert a moral eclipse by observances and noises differing in kind only from that clashing of pots and pans still made by certain African tribes to keep off an eclipse of the moon. The *Spectator* says that every accurate thinker will see at once, that free will, Providence, and Miracles do not differ in *principle* at all, but are only *more* or *less* startling results of the same *facts*." In this, I believe, every "accurate thinker" among the Necessitarians will be disposed perfectly to agree with him.

In the *Spectator* of the following week (February 3,) we have another writer on the same subject in a notice of Dr. Travis and Sir William Hamilton. Dr. Travis in "Moral Freedom Reconciled with Causation", lays down the rather startling proposition that acts may be *self*-determined while they are *caused* by something else, a position rather difficult to reconcile with the ordinary use of logic. Although, says the Dr., we cannot control the affections acting upon our organization at any particular moment, we may indefinitely increase or diminish the force of any one, by *dwelling* or *refusing to dwell* upon the thoughts adapted to keep it before our minds. By this spontaneous power, says Dr. Travis, man can gradually mould his character, and is therefore

wrong, virtue and vice, having no existence but as they affect the wellbeing of the sentient creation. Truth, justice, and wisdom are only relations to finite things, and cannot therefore be infinite or absolute in their own nature.

In the natural world we have strong likes and antipathies, and we call some things nice and others nasty, as they affect us pleasurably or the reverse, but on examination we find

---

a free agent, not in the sense of being able to withdraw himself from the law of causality, but because these acts of attention are one of the causes by which his character at any particular instant is formed. Now, as the Dr. admits that there is "a cause for dwelling or refusing to dwell" and that the *spontaneous* power is under causality, the difference between him and the necessitarians is evidently a distinction without a difference. "To make Dr. Travis's position thoroughly defensible, (says E. V. N.,) we require to show that there is some internal principle of action belonging to our minds, which accounts for our acts of attention without recourse to any external motive. We think that such a principle may be proved to exist, by the fact that *what the mind takes to pieces it has always first put together*, that the reflections of thought always relate to previous constructions of the imagination. Our space forbids our doing more than state this principle, which, simple as it may appear, nevertheless casts a marvellous light on many of the obscurest questions of metaphysics, not least on this question of the freedom of the will. Construction implies selection and arrangement. Now these are essentially free acts, because they involve the power of rejection. The bird chooses and combines the materials for its nest according to an idea supplied by its own mind, throwing aside those unsuitable to its purpose. The range of selection may be limited, but within these limits its choice is free. Now in man this constructive power is unlimited. His imagination determines alike ends and means, under the guidance of principles admitting the widest scope, ideas of utility, beauty, harmony, unity, &c. If the will which sways such a faculty is not free, what does freedom mean?" What indeed! I should say the absence of any possibility of either reason or science, both of which are built on "law." The very words selection, and arrangement, and rejection, imply a reason for their exercise, that is a *governing* power to the will.—The bird even has its own reasons for what he does,

them all composed of the same simple elements of oxygen, hydrogen, and carbon; and the same simple forces, or their correlates, acting through different parts of the brain, produce all the phenomena of the moral world. If we love the rose and avoid assafœtida it is not from any supposed free will in the rose to smell sweet and look beautiful, but because its attributes affect us pleasurably. It is the same in the moral world, we judge of things as they affect us, and of people by their attributes. We put the human rose in our bosom, and we avoid the ugly and disagreeable person as we would assafœtida, and for the same reason. We cannot love that which is disagreeable because we know it did not make itself, and the merit we ascribe both to things and persons is according to qualities or attributes without reference to the fact that all qualities are derived. Upon these affections and antipathies, upon our likes and dislikes, our moral systems have been formed,—calling that good which affects us pleasurably, and that evil which affects us painfully. It is true we have called things by very high sounding names, and have gone up to Heaven and down to Hell to aid us in force of expression, but the truth of this simple position has not been in the least affected, it has

---

limited we are told, while man's constructive power is unlimited. It may have "the widest scope" but unless it is infinite it cannot be unlimited. It seems that according to E. V. N.'s new principle, of which I am sorry he cannot tell us more, the will aways the determining power, not the determining power the will. It does not matter whether it is an "internal principle of action," or "external motive," that governs the will, and the acts dependent upon it, so that it is governed. Reasonable motive ought to govern the will, and the nearer we approach the madman and the idiot the nearer we get to freedom; not that any one, unless it be the *Spectator*, supposes even their acts or volitions to be uncaused.

only been obscured by thus putting words in the place of things. Language is a most imperfect instrument for the expression of ideas, even with the most philosophical; with the many the names are a part of the things themselves; and as things were named when they were imperfectly known, errors are retained and perpetuated from generation to generation. "All moral rules are derived originally from utility, but the pleasures and pains, or likes and antipathies on which they are based are transmitted to offspring and thus become intuitions, similar to the feelings with which the kitten regards a dog; it sets up its back and spits at it directly it opens its eyes; the cow also from the same cause, from its having been the custom years ago to bait her forefathers, keeps making imaginary tosses of the dog, whenever she sees one; and the bull himself is still made furious by the sight of a red colour, although the feeling may have been derived ages ago in the bull-fights of Spain. In this way are mixed the tendencies of actions and the feelings with which in a long course of time we intuitively come to regard them, and their original source is thus sometimes lost. What is called the Intuitive School of Moralists—bases its conclusions partly on utility, and partly on such internal convictions, for which no reason can be assigned, except a certain feeling on the subject, and which usually takes the shape of 'all men think,' 'we cannot help feeling,' &c. To recognize however, the obligations of morality is simply to recognize the conditions on which it is desirable men should live, and the authority is enforced by pains and penalties which all are forced to attend to whether the obligations are recognized and acknowledged or not.

"It is often said that it is impossible to speak definitely of the objects of creation, that happiness is not a sufficiently worthy object, but that development seems more the end and aim of the Creator than happiness. But what is the use of 'development' unless attended by consciousness, and that a pleasurable consciousness? a painful consciousness would be worse than nothing. World on world in infinite beauty would be the same as none without beings conscious of their existence, and unless that beauty gave pleasure—a happy consciousness,—it would be useless. Were a universe developed in all possible power and beauty and but one little fly conscious of its existence, that little fly would be of vastly more importance than the universe. Beings might be 'developed' in infinite number, size, and power, but of what use would their existence be if they were not happy, or at least a source of happiness? Pain checks development, and all legitimate development is attended with pleasure, and, in fact, we can see no good in development unless it produces happiness. We cannot see or even understand any other purpose in creation: to be without consciousness is the same as not being; and consciousness that was neither pleasurable nor painful would be no consciousness, for there is no negation or state of indifference, no sensation, or feeling, or idea, attending either the intellect or sentiments that is not slightly either one or the other. Certainly pain would not be worth living for, and happiness is the only thing left. People speak of pleasure with contempt, because by it is usually meant something carnal and resulting from the lower feelings, but happiness *is simply the aggregate of pleasurable sensation from whatever source derived:* again, you hear people decry happiness as poor and paltry, as something scarcely worth having, and speak of blessedness as the end to be attained; but by blessedness they evidently mean a refined kind of happiness, composed principally of the religious and æsthetic feelings. We hear much also in the present day of 'Law, Order, and Unity;' but law, order and unity, that serve no purpose, are no evidence of wisdom of design.' * * * The obligation, then, that a man is under to act in one way rather than in another, is owing to its tendency to happiness or to the avoidance of pain, and Morality may be defined as the 'the science which teaches man to live together in the most happy manner possible.'—(*Helvetius*.)" * Bentham says, "No man ever had, can, or could have a motive differing from the pursuit of pleasure or the avoidance of pain."

J. S. Mill says, "A volition is a moral effect, which follows the corresponding moral causes as certainly and invariably as physical effects follow their physical causes." To present these moral causes then is the object of the moralist. "To prove that the immoral action is a miscalculation of self-interest; to show how erroneous an estimate the vicious man makes of pains and pleasures, is the purpose of the intelligent moralist."—*Bentham*. Man's freedom consists in being able to do as he pleases, which is all-sufficient; the object then must be to present such motives as will make him please to do that which will be most for the lasting interest of himself and society.

MORAL RESPONSIBILITY.—But if no action of our lives in the then state of our minds, and the circumstances in which we were placed, could have been different, what becomes of our Accountability or Responsibility? It consists in the consequences of our actions, which are pleasurable or painful as they are right or wrong, that is, as they tend to benefit or injure ourselves or society. It is for the moralist then to guard, and if necessary to increase, these pains and pleasures, and as man necessarily seeks that which is pleasurable and avoids that which is painful, the interests of

* Philosophy of Necessity, p. 87 to 89-90.

morality are sufficiently assured. But if all actions are the same, *per se*, and could not possibly have been otherwise under the circumstances, what have we to preach about? What becomes of sin and iniquity, &c.? All that may be safely buried, and all we have to do in morals as in physics, is to show the consequences of our actions. The laws of morality are as fixed, and determinate, and unvarying, as are those that keep the planets in their sphere.

The common and erroneous idea of Responsibilty—of man's being an accountable agent—is the rightfulness of inflicting punishment, that is, of apportioning a certain amount of suffering to a certain amount of sin, which he is supposed to have *deserved* because he could have done differently; but as this is not the case—as he could *not* have acted differently, all responsibility in this sense would be unjust, and as such actions are already past and could not be recalled, it would be as useless as unjust. The pains and penalties, or punishments, attending our actions, are for our good; to show us when we have done wrong, that is, done that which will injure us; and to prevent our doing it again; and we are so punished whether our actions are voluntary or not, that is, whether they are what is called free, or merely accidental. Whether we fall into the fire or put ourselves in voluntarily, the pain is the same, the object being to make us get out again as soon as possible and thus avert the consequences of being burned. It is the same in other penalties, whether the pains are those of conscience or merely bodily. Forgiveness of sins then, or to be relieved from that punishment which is for our good, would be simply doing us an injury,—and not to forgive, if no good comes from punishment, would be mere vengeance. The myriads of human beings whom, *it is said*, God has "fore-ordained," that is, designed beforehand, to be punished to all eternity, "to the praise of his glorious justice," as the Westminster Confession has it*, may consistently with that justice be safely released. Moral Responsibility, so much contended for, is merely the supposed *right* to take *revenge* for injuries done to us.

* See also the sermon of Jonathan Edwards, the unanswerable champion of Philosophical Necessity, on the "Justice of God in the damnation of Sinners," and the diary of Mr. Carey on the "pleasure" and "sweetness" he had experienced in reading that sermon.

Surely Free Will would be a most undesirable gift if accompanied by such possible consequences; surely God could never make his creatures "free" thus to injure themselves irretrievably! Infinite power and benevolence and eternal punishments are contradictions. But men are better than their creeds, they do not realize or really believe this horrid dogma; if they did it would put a stop to all action in this world —who could go about his daily work with such a possible doom hanging over him? or who but a selfish brute beast, acting upon mere brute instinct, would dare to bring children into the world whose possible and even probable fate was endless torment. To me it appears the blackest libel on the name of the Creator that Hell itself could invent, and wherever we find that the doctrine is received in any seriousness, it has, as we might expect, the most brutalizing tendency. Mr. Lecky, in his History of Rationalism, shows how completely this effect was produced in Scotland in the sixteenth century, in the torturing and burning of supposed witches, and in persecution generally. He says :—
" The Reformed clergy all over Scotland applauded and stimulated the persecution. The ascendancy they had obtained was boundless; and in this respect their power was entirely undisputed. One word from them might have arrested the tortures, but that word was never spoken. Their conduct implies not merely a mental aberration, but also a callousness of feeling which has rarely been attained in a long career of vice. Yet these were men who had often shown, in the most trying circumstances, the highest and the most heroic virtue. They were men whose courage had never flinched when persecution was raging around—men who had never paltered with their consciences to attain the favour of a king—men whose self-devotion and zeal in their sacred calling had seldom been surpassed—men who, in all the private relations of life, were doubtless amiable and affectionate. It is not on them that our blame should fall: it is on the system that made them what they were. They were but illustrations of the great truth, that when men have come to regard a certain class of their fellow creatures

As motives govern our volitions, we praise or blame, reward or punish, as motives to induce one line of conduct rather than another. A man who sets up his free will and refuses to be *governed* by motives is either a madman or a fool, and his actions are not the less caused. If a man could refuse to be governed by the strongest motive, all moral influences, and praise and blame, would be useless, and all reasoning upon his conduct impossible, for we should never be able to predict what he would do from what he had done. We judge of *acts* by their tendency; but as all mental action originates in motives, it is by motives that *character* must be judged, and an act is moral, not because it is free, but because it arises in moral motives.

---

as doomed by the Almighty to eternal and excruciating agonies, and when their theology directs their minds with intense and realising earnestness to the contemplation of such agonies, the result will be an indifference to the suffering of those whom they deem the enemies of their God, as absolute as it is perhaps possible for human nature to attain." Of course under such a dogma, if only half believed, intolerance and persecution become the highest duty, and all human sympathy must be made to stand aside. The Spaniards, with their Inquisition, and the Scotch, only showed that they were more earnest in their belief than other nations who professed to hold the same faith. Mr. Lecky says, " If men believe with an intense and untiring faith that their own view of a disputed question is true beyond all possibility of mistake—if they further believe that those who adopt other views will be doomed by the Almighty to an eternity of misery, which with the same moral desperation, but with a different belief, they would have escaped,—these men will, sooner or later, persecute to the extent of their power. If you speak to them of the physical and moral sufferings which persecution produces, or of the sincerity and unselfish heroism of its victims, they will reply that such arguments rest altogether on the inadequacy of your realisation of the doctrine they believe—what suffering that men can inflict can be comparable to the eternal misery of all who embrace the doctrine of the heretic? what claim can human virtues have to our forbearance, if the Almighty punishes the mere profession of error as a crime of the deepest turpitude?"

CHAPTER III.

UPON THAT WHICH UNDERLIES ALL PHENOMENA.

> "And what if all of animated nature
> Be but organic harps diversely framed,
> That tremble into thought, as over them sweeps,
> Plastic and vast, one intellectual breeze,
> At once the soul of each, and God of all?"
> *Coleridge.*

> "Then shall the dust return to the earth as it was: and the spirit shall return to God who gave it."—*Ecclesiastes.*

> "In all phenomena the more closely they are investigated the more we are convinced that, humanly speaking, neither matter nor force can be created or annihilated, and that an essential cause is unattainable.— Causation is the will, Creation the act of God."—*W. R. Grove.* Correlation of Physical Forces.

WE should have no grounds for supposing that matter existed if matter did not exert force, and the popular idea is, that matter could be separated from this force, or from its manifestations or *accidents*, and that the laws which govern matter are external to itself. But, as we have seen, it is most probable that the force, or manifestations, or *accidents*, or laws, are all that really exists.

Our faculties make us acquainted with qualities or attributes without ourselves, and we assume that these must be qualities or attributes of *something*, and we have called it Matter; we have feelings and ideas, and we equally assume that they also must belong to something, and we call it

Mind; but there is in reality nothing to which these mental and physical attributes belong, they exist *per se* as force and its correlates. THERE IS NOTHING UNDERLYING PHENOMENA—PHENOMENA ARE CORRELATES OF FORCE, AND FORCE IS ALL. When we speak of Qualities, we indicate only how we are affected by Force external; vital force is the correlate of this physical force; and ideas and feelings are the correlate of vital force, not existing in anything, but each idea or feeling existing separately; and when it ceases to exist as an idea or feeling, it merely takes some other form, and is still persistent. What form it may possibly take we shall speculate upon in another chapter. Hume says, "Since all our perceptions are different from each other, and from everything else in the universe, they are also distinct and separable, and may be considered as separably existent, and may exist separately, and have no need of anything else to support their existence." And again, "We have no perfect idea of anything but a perception. A substance is entirely different from a perception. We have therefore no idea of a substance. Inhesion in something is supposed to be requisite to support the existence of our perceptions. Nothing appears requisite to support the existence of our perceptions. We have therefore no idea of inhesion. What possibility, then, of answering that question, *Whether perceptions inhere in a material or immaterial substance*, when we do not so much as understand the meaning of the question?" * It would appear then, that that which underlies phenomena, and the phenomena—the noumenon and the phenomenon—the non-ego and the ego—in their Inmost Nature are the same; that is, "Mind and Matter are only phenomenal modifications of the same common substance," viz., of force. This is the true doctrine of

* A Treatise of Human Nature, vol. I., p. 311, et. seq.

"Absolute Identity," taught in another form by Schelling, Hegel, and Cousin. "There is no fact," says Fichte, "no Tree there, but only a manifestation of Power from something that is *not I*,"—that is, a certain amount of force was received into the system, and, meeting other forces from without, was changed into that compound idea called a tree, and having done that, would pass into some other form or modification. There is not, however, an Absolute Identity between the external power and the idea of the tree, since to complete the idea other powers are supplied from within, or from the ego. The thing known and the mind knowing are one in quality or essence, but not in quantity.

We find then but one thing in the world,—Force; and what is that? Force and Power are the same, and Power we cannot separate from that source of all power,—from God,— Power is God. We say the power of God, as if it could be separated from Him, or delegated; but this is clearly inconceivable. The one only thing we find anywhere is God.

The fundamental principle in the doctrine of Spinoza is the simplicity of the Universe, and the unity of that substance, in which he supposes both thought and matter to inhere. He says, "Whatever we discover externally by sensation; whatever we feel internally by reflection; all these are nothing but modifications of that one simple and necessarily existent being, and are not possessed of any separate and distinct existence."* "There is but one infinite Substance, and that is God. Whatever is, is in God; and without Him nothing can be conceived. He is the universal Being of which all things are the manifestations. * * * Extension and Thought are the objective and subjective, of which God is the Identity. Every *thing* is a mode of God's attribute of Extension; every *thought*, wish, or feeling, a mode

* Hume on Human Nature, vol. L, p. 319.

E

of his attribute of Thought. * * * God is the one 'idea immanens'—the One and All."*

The one infinite Substance and the "Force" of our modern Scientific conceptions are identical, and the question is, what do we and can we actually know of it? First, then, Science shows its Unity. "The simplest germination of a lichen is," says Lewes, "if we apprehend it rightly, directly linked with the grandest astronomical phenomena; nor could an infusory animalcule be annihilated without altering the equilibrium of the universe. Plato had some forecast of this when he taught that the world was a great animal; and others, since Plato, when they considered the universe the manifestation of some transcendent life, with which every separate individual life was related, as parts are to the whole." Emerson says, "Every thing in nature contains all the powers of nature; everything is made of one hidden stuff. The true doctrine of Omnipresence is, that God re-appears in all his parts, in every moss and cobweb; thus the Universe is alive."

The Rev. J. White Mailler, M.A., says, "When we view the world as one universal effect, we are at once led to the contemplation of a universal Divine Agency. Does not the Infinite act on every atom? God never delegates his power; He cannot transfer divinity to a substance: there is no power therefore separate from Himself. In Him all things have their being."†

Science, then, proves the Unity of Force; throughout the Universe, as far as our observation extends, every atom is pulling at every other atom; it also equally shows that it is not what we call dead, passive, or blind force, but universally active and intelligent, that is, it partakes of the attributes which

* Lewes' History of Philosophy, vol. III., p. 146.
† The Philosophy of the Bible, pp. 55 and 40.

we ascribe only to mind. If the One simple, homogeneous substance or force did not partake of the nature of mind, what could *at first* have originated change in it? whereas we now know it to be the cause of all things, and that all those changes tend to definite purposes. We are accustomed only to ascribe Intelligence to sensitive beings, whereas every atom is equally intelligent and tending towards a given purpose*, and one is no more an independent agency than the other, for all things that *begin to be*, whether in mind or matter, must have a cause why they begin to be, and they are not therefore self-existent, but the foundation of their existence must be *without* themselves, and the intelligence shown in either mind or atom is no part of either, but is something separate and beyond. There is nothing in nature exercising an independent agency. A cause must be uncaused; if produced as all things around us by the persistence of force, it is an effect. There can be only one cause, therefore, and all the rest are passive results.

All things in nature being thus derived, the original from which they are derived must exist somewhere.

This is what we call the Great First Cause.

"The meaning of a First Cause is, (says Mill,) that all other things exist, and are what they are by reason of it

---

* "There lies all the difficulties about these atoms. These same 'relations' in which they stand to one another are anything but simple ones. They involve all the 'ologies' and all the 'ometries,' and in these days we know something of what that implies. Their movements, their interchanges, their 'hates and loves,' their 'attractions and repulsions,' their 'correlations,' their what not, are all determined on the very instant. There is no hesitation, no blundering, no trial and error. * * * The *presence* of MIND is what solves the whole difficulty; so far, at least, as it brings it within the sphere of our own consciousness, and into conformity with our own experience of what action is."—*Sir J. F. W. Herschel.*

and of its properties, but that it is not itself made to exist, nor to be what it is, by anything else. It does not depend for its existence or attributes, on other things: there is nothing upon the existence of which its own is conditional: it exists absolutely." *

But there are those who say that there is no First Cause, but that the chain of causation goes back to all eternity—an infinite non-commencement. They assert that qualities and properties and attributes are *inherent*, that they have *always* existed, and they see no evidence of purpose or design in creation, but think that in the infinite concourse and commingling of atoms or forces in infinite time and space, the present order of things has arisen; everything inharmonious having a natural and necessary tendency to destroy itself, and only that which is good and harmonious being permanent or having power to continue in existence at all. But even supposing qualities to be inherent, and laws, or the longest observed order of facts, to be necessary and permanent, still it is difficult to see how anything but chance could result from the joint action of one set of laws upon another, if force were blind. It is with results, and not with the primary laws or qualities that we have to do. Sir John Herschel tells us, that "among all the *possible combinations* of the fifty or sixty elements which chemistry points to as existing on this earth, that some have never yet been formed" and who can say, when such combination does take place what the result will be? It may take a million chances to effect one purpose—an almost infinite series to bring about one reciprocity, and then one more turn of the *necessary* screw—one adverse combination, might take us back to chaos. "No one law determines anything that we see happening or done around us. It is

* Mill on Hamilton, p. 86.

always the result of differing or opposing forces nicely balanced against each other. The least disturbance of the proportion in which any one of them is allowed to tell, produces a total change in the effect. The more we know of nature, the more intricate do such combinations appear to be. The existence of laws, therefore, is not the end of our physical knowledge. What we always reach at last in the course of every physical inquiry, is the recognition, not of individual laws, but of some definite relation to each other, in which different laws are placed, so as to bring about a particular result. But this is, in other words, the principle of adjustment, and adjustment has no meaning except as the instrument and the result of purpose. * * * The motion of the earth might be exactly what it is, every fact in respect to our planetary position might remain unchanged, yet the seasons would return in vain if our own atmosphere were altered in any one of the elements of its composition, or if any one of the laws regulating its action were other than it is. Under a thinner air even the torrid zone might be wrapped in eternal snow. Under a denser air, and one with different refracting powers, the earth and all that is therein might be burnt up. * * * Then, the relations in which these inorganic compounds stand to the chemistry of life, constitute another vast series in which the principle of adjustment has applications infinite in number, and as infinite in beauty. How delicate these relations are, and how tremendous are the issues depending on their management, may be conceived from a single fact. The same elements combined in one proportion are sometimes a nutritious food or a grateful stimulant, soothing and sustaining the powers of life; whilst, combined in another proportion, they may be a deadly poison, paralysing the heart and carrying agony along every nerve and fibre of the animal frame. This is no mere theoretical possibility. It is actually the relation in which two well-known substances stand to each other—Tea and Strychnia. The active principle of these two substances, "Theine" and "Strychnine," are identical so far as their elements are concerned, and differ from each other only in the proportions in which they are combined. Such is the power of numbers in the laboratory of Nature! What havoc in this world, so full of life, would be made by blind chance gambling with such powers as those!"* It is impossible to conceive that inherent forces working blindly could produce the unity of purpose we everywhere see, or if by a million chances to one they did, what is to secure its permanence? Were properties *inherent*, then it would be impossible to escape the conviction that there is a higher force controlling their individual tendencies; but recent science shows that there is nothing inherent: the very name itself implies that such forces are inherited or derived. The force, or rather "form", in an acorn, by which it can only become an oak, or the difference between an acorn and the seed of a scarlet runner or a gourd, is, as we have seen, dependent upon organisation, which is derived from the parent stock. Even what we call properties, and which are assumed to be inherent, are, as we have seen, formed in the mind itself, the result of organization. The law of the Persistence of Force and the law of Evolution are the same. Every existing state has grown out of the preceding, and all its forces have been used up in present phenomena, the change from physical to sentient and mental greatly increasing with each succeeding age; as Oersted says, "Everything that exists depends upon the past, prepares the future, and is related to the whole."

* The Reign of Law. By the Duke of Argyle.—*Good Words*.

Comte is of opinion that, when properly converted to the positive mode of thought, "mankind will cease to refer the constitution of Nature to an intelligent will and Supreme Governor of the world;" on the contrary, Science finds only a universe of effects,—nothing is what it is in itself, everything is derived; the Universal Cause is everywhere without, not inherent, and what we see the Vital Force is to the Acorn, we may suppose God is to the Universe.

Oersted says, "The world is governed by an eternal reason, which makes known to us its actions by unalterable laws."

It is true the Laws of Nature are unalterable, but is the connection between each cause and effect a necessary one, or dependent only upon the volition of the Eternal Reason? Those who believe in inherent properties believe also in an indissoluble necessary connection. But Hume is supposed to have clearly shown that there is no proof whatever of any necessary connection; but that all we know and can speak of is the invariableness; and J. S. Mill says, "What experience makes known, is the fact of the invariable sequence between every event and some special combination of antecedent conditions, in such sort that wherever and whenever that union of antecedents exists, the event does not fail to occur. Any *must* in this case, any necessity, other than the unconditional universality of the fact, we know nothing of." And again, "Whether it *must* do so, I acknowledge myself to be entirely ignorant, be the phenomenon moral or physical; and I condemn, accordingly, the word Necessity as applied to either case. All I know is, that it always *does*."* But if we can show why it always does; that the connection is a moral rather than a physical one; then I think the higher probability is that such invariable connection has been established to answer a special purpose, and is not necessary, but in other

* Examination of Sir William Hamilton's Philosophy, pp. 500, 501.

circumstances might be dissolved. All the purposes in creation evidently point to one object—the production of the largest amount of sensitive existence. The whole surface of the earth is one net-work of nerves, so that, as in the human body, so in the body of the world, you can scarcely insert the point of a needle where there is no sentience. Life is always preserved at a high pressure. "There is no exception to the rule," says Darwin, "that every organic being naturally increases at so high a rate, that if not destroyed, this earth would soon be covered by the progeny of a single pair." Without respect to individuals, the object seems to be to keep the greatest number possible in the best possible state for enjoyment:—

> "So careful of the type she seems,
> So careless of the single life."

Now the enjoyment, and indeed we may say the existence of this mass of life, depends upon the uniformity of nature's laws. The exercise of the highest reasoning power in man, equally with the lowest instinct of the brute, depends upon the order of nature to-day being as yesterday; upon the being able to calculate what will be from what has been; upon the delicate relationship between instinct and object being sustained. It has been said "That the testimony of consciousness must be believed, because to disbelieve it, would be to impute mendacity and perfidy to the Creator," but Locke truly observes, "How short soever our knowledge may be of a universal or perfect comprehension of whatever is, it yet secures our great concernments," and that "God has given us assurance enough as to the existence of things without us; since by their different application we can produce in ourselves both pleasure and pain." In fact in whatever way the world is created within us, and however far short our consciousness may come of absolute truth, our relation to the outer world is quite sufficient to guide us to the objects of our desires, upon the gratification of which our happiness depends; our consciousness is therefore no deception, but all that is necessary, and all that it was intended to be; but if after attaining that knowledge of the "order of nature," upon which our safety and wellbeing depended, that order were changed, or altered, or interfered with, by what is called Free Will, or a special Providence, that would certainly be a breach of faith. Whether then the connection between cause and effect in the order of nature be a necessary one, or mere invariable antecedence and consequence, it is certainly desirable for all the purposes of life that such connection should be unaltered and unalterable,—it is therefore most probably established and maintained by the Will of the Creator;—based upon the volition of the Absolute.

We find, then, but one infinite Substance, and that is the same with the Force or Power we see everywhere around us. We find only Force changing into Life, and Life into Sentience—a great aggregated pleasurable Consciousness guarded by pain. Death and Birth are the great waste and reproductive system of this great Sentient body, and the one is as necessary as the other, as Death may be said to be the Parent of Life.* Advancing Science shows that the Cosmos, both sentient and insentient, is one and indivisible, and viewed in this light, as a whole it is ever progressing towards increasing happiness. By the Natural law of Progress, called "Natural Selection," the weak and bad and ugly are constantly making room for the strong and good and beautiful. Pleasure is the rule, pain the exception, and the aggregate of

* "There is no death in the concrete, what passes away passes away into its own self—only the passing away passes away. The consciousness abides—the essential being is."—*Hegel.*

pleasurable sensation constitutes happiness, and this taken as a whole must be sufficient completely to obliterate the pain, which man calls evil.*

Thus the warp and woof of the Mind of God may be made up of the totality of the individual threads of consciousness, extending through the countless worlds of which this is a mere speck—a grain of sand. "The phenomenal is the life of the Absolute." I am not disposed, therefore, to join men of science in their Altar to "The Unknown and Unknowable God," because I cannot separate God from

* Man in judging of the purposes of creation and of what he calls evil, confines his strictures either to himself individually, or at the widest range to that of the human race. In both he errs, he must take in the whole of sentient existence. Theodore Parker supplies an admirable illustration of this limitation of our view. Thus, "An oak tree in the woods appears quite perfect. The leaves are coiled up and spoiled by the leaf-roller; eat to pieces by the tailor beetle; eaten by the hay-moth and the polyphemus, the slug, caterpillar, and her numerous kindred; the twigs are sucked by the white-lined tree-hopper, or cut off by the oak-pruner; large limbs are broken down by the seventeen-year locust; the horn-bug, the curculio, and the timber-beetle, eat up its wood; the gadfly punctures leaf and bark, converting the forces of the tree to that insect's use; the grub lies in the young acorn; flycatchers are on its leaves; a spider weaves its web from twig to twig; caterpillars of various denominations gnaw its tender shoots; the creeper and the wood-pecker bore through the bark; squirrels, striped, flying, red, and grey, have gnawed into its limbs, and made their nests; the toad has a hole in a flaw in its base; the fox has cut asunder its fibrous roots in digging his burrow; the bear dwells in its trunk, which worms, emmets, bees, and countless insects have helped to hollow; ice and the winds of winter have broken off full many a bough. How imperfect and incomplete the oak tree looks, so broken, gnarled, and grim! ... But it has served its complicated purpose; ... no doubt, the good God is quite content with His oak, and says: 'Well done, good and faithful servant!'

"We commonly look on the world as the carpenter and millwright on that crooked oak; and because it does not serve our turn completely, we think it an imperfect world."

Nature, but believe that what we can learn of one, we know also of the other: I would simply transfer our Theology, as distinguished from Religion, from the Pulpit to the Lecture-room. Our Priests must be one with our men of science, our Prophets are the Poets: their Inspiration tells us truly that:—

> "All are but parts of one stupendous whole,
> Whose body nature is, and God the soul."

> "These as they change, Almighty Father, these,
> Are but the varied God."
>
> * * * * *
>
> "But wandering oft, with brute unconscious gaze,
> Man marks not thee," &c.

To him who thus "sees God in clouds and hears him in the wind," who cannot separate Him from one atom of the living universe of which he is the author and supporter, the orthodox, but ignorant disparagement of this beautiful world, appears impious, libellous, and above all things ungrateful.

On this subject the ancient Hindoo and Greek mind arrived at the same results. They came to the conclusion, as we learn from the profound and condensed work of Dr. J. W. Draper, that the world is a manifestation of God, emanating from Him, and being re-absorbed into Him again; they held also, that the soul is immortal, but as it issued from the Deity so would it be re-absorbed. "As a drop of water pursues a devious course in the cloud, in the rain, in the river, a part of a plant, or a part of an animal, but sooner or later inevitably finds its way back to the sea from which it came, so the soul, however various its fortunes may have been, sinks back at last into the Divinity from which it emanated." A little rivulet of force has been taken from the general ocean to turn our little mill; it again hastens back to regain its source, again and again to be raised by the Great Sun to go its round as before. Man's early intuitions made him feel that everything was the work of the Great Spirit; now his intuitions, generally so right at first, are obscured by secondary causes which he calls science and laws of nature; and thus "Nature, which is the Time-vesture of God, and reveals Him to the wise, hides Him from the foolish." *

* The following letter from Mr. H. G. Atkinson, F.G.S., which I have permission to insert, may I think interest many of my readers:—

"I have been deep into the mystery of things this morning—comparing Plato with the Kabbalah. One thing occurs to me as fundamental to almost all religious schemes and principles of faith, including the modern spiritualists, that the form of the faith or creed is little more than a mere reflex of the course of nature as we observe it about us and within us. At one time we have a God representing the first principles of things, as a man—or an architect framing the universe—and Father of all mankind. And again, the Great First Cause is proclaimed to be a profound mystery and hidden secret. The unknown and unknowable of philosophers and men of science—and the En Soph of the Kabbalah, and inconceivable Trinity in Unity of the Christian—representing the secret subtle source or principle of action and formative power in nature. And even could we discover the nature of God, says Plato, it would be impossible to explain it; and yet he tells you that God is mind acting upon matter, somewhat after the manner of a watchmaker making a watch—the intractible nature of the material being the origin of evil; with arguments for the immortality of the soul, not very logically convincing. But in the Kabbalah we have the original cause without mind, representing insensible matter, from out of which mind develops. Now these different ideas do but reflect the form and nature of things about us. The fact and process of observed natural action either in respect to our own nature or the nature without us, and in a roundabout way we have simply emanations falling back again upon their source, and as in the Kabbalah and with the Buddhist, a longing for peace in rest and eternal sleep—a re-absorption, and in fact annihilation as the end most devoutly to be wished; in fact the getting quit of ourselves as a very good riddance to bad rubbish, and which is actually the sum and substance of the pervading idea of the Buddhist religion. And the notion forcibly presents itself to my mind, that it is the tendency under an

NATURE AN INFINITELY DIVIDED GOD.

The highest minds seem everywhere to have come, by very different roads, very much to similar conclusions: thus Schelling says, "The world is but a balancing of contending powers within the sphere of the absolute." The Ego in Fechte's system is a finite Ego—it is the human soul. In Schiller's it is the Absolute—the Infinite—the all which Spinoza called Substance; and this Absolute manifests itself in two forms: in the form of the Ego and in the form of the Non-Ego—as Nature and as Mind. The Ego produces the Non-Ego, but not by its own force, not out of its own nature; it is the universal Nature which works within us and which produces from out of us; it is the universal Nature which here is conscious of itself. Men are but the innumerable individual eyes with which the Infinite World-spirit beholds himself.* Schiller says "Nature is an infinitely

---

ignorance of real causes and the sources of particular effects, to mistake—(as in the belief in ghosts and spirits,—extraneous or sympathetic) the effects for causes, and hence we have the affections ascribed to the heart, and called heart to this day; whilst the actor upon the stage still puts his hand to his heart as a natural action in the expression of the warmth of his affections, though no such action is ever observed in real life. Plato plants 'the irascible passions which originate in pride and resentment,' in the breast, because under their action sensations are experienced in that region; 'the love of pleasure or concupiscent part of the soul,' he seats in the belly and inferior parts of the body', taking the means for the origin or 'final cause', &c.; but in placing the reasoning and judging powers in the head as 'a firm citadel, and of which the senses are its guides and servants,' he was right, because every man is sensible of the fact now verified by so many other tests and reasons; and without being misled by the sympathy with other parts of the system. To collect, analyse, and record all such specious notions and speculative anticipations—misleading illusions of long ages of error, before the true principles of a real science burst upon us, is extremely interesting and profoundly instructive."

* Lewes's Biographical History of Philosophy, vol. iv., p. 199.

divided God," and again, "The Divine One has dispersed itself into innumerable sensible substances, as a white beam of light is decomposed by the prism into seven coloured rays. And a divine being would be evolved from the union of all these substances, as the seven coloured rays dissolve again into the clear-light beam. The existing form of nature is the optic glass, and all the activities of spirit are only an infinite colour-play of that simple divine ray. Should it ever please the Almighty to shatter this prism, then the barrier between himself and the world would fall to ruin; all spirits would disappear into one infinite spirit, all accords would melt into one harmony, all streams would rest in one ocean. The attraction of the elements gave to nature its material form. The attraction of spirits, multiplied and continued to infinity, must finally lead to the abolition of the separation, or (may I utter it,) create God."*

The Universe, according to Hegel, is a thought, a beat, a pulse, of the Absolute Mind. * * * In the minutest act of our mind is the same secret—logical, physical, metaphysical—as in the entire Universe.† And again, "Being underlies all modes and forms of being," and in creation, "Being—Becomes." Emerson says, "Everything in nature contains all the powers of nature; everything is made of one hidden stuff. The true doctrine of Omnipresence is, that God reappears in all his parts in every moss and cobweb; thus the universe is alive."‡ Theodore Parker says, "If God be Infinite, then he must be imminent, perfectly and totally present in Nature and in Spirit. Thus there is no point in space, no atom of matter, but God is there; no point of spirit, no atom of soul, but God is there. And yet finite matter and finite

* Philosophical Letter, p. 40.
† Masson's Recent British Philosophy, p. 279.
‡ Essay on Compensation.

spirit do not exhaust God. He transcends the world of matter and of spirit; and in virtue of that transcendence continually makes the world of matter fairer, and the world of spirit wiser. So there is really a progress in the manifestation of God, not a progress in God the manifesting." Professor Ferrier, of St. Andrew's, says, "All absolute existences are contingent *except one*; in other words, there is One, but only one, Absolute Existence which is strictly *necessary*; and that existence is a supreme and infinite and everlasting Mind in synthesis with all things." *

Carlyle also:—"This fair universe, in the meanest province thereof, is in very deed the star-domed City of God; through every star, through every grass-blade, and most through every living soul, the glory of a present God still beams: But Nature, which is the Time-vesture of God, and reveals Him to the wise, hides Him from the foolish." †

The Christian doctrine is, that "In Him (God) we live and move and have our being." That God is all in all, and the Devil something besides, is only the *unanswerable* logic of the pulpit. ‡

---

* Institutes of Metaphysics: The Theory of Knowing and Being.
† Sartor Resartus, p. 274.
‡ We are told repeatedly by those who support this influence or personage that we are not to rest in second causes, and yet they make the Devil the "Origin of Evil" and not his Maker. The fact is that a Being who is always in pursuit of pain, that is, of evil, who, with above ordinary intelligence, is always systematically acting in opposition to his own interest, is an impossibility. We know of no creature who is not seeking the greatest *apparent* good, in the "pursuit of pleasure or the avoidance of pain." God is the Great First Cause—the Author of all things, and if He could have made a world like this earth, with all the happiness it now contains, without pain, no doubt he would have done so. We must limit either His Goodness or His Power, and we prefer the latter, as it is not derogatory to the character of God that he cannot perform impossibilities. He could not make that not to have

The Duke of Argyle, in the admirable paper on the Reign of Law, from which we have already quoted, says:—"Science, in the modern doctrine of the Conservation of Energy, and Convertibility of Forces, is already getting something like a firm hold of the idea that all kinds of force are but forms and manifestations of some one central Force, issuing from some one fountain-head of power. Sir John Herschel has not hesitated to say that 'it is but reasonable to regard the force of gravitation as the direct or indirect result of a consciousness and a will existing somewhere.' And even if we cannot assume that force, in all its forms, is due to the direct working of the Creator, at least let us not think or speak of the forces of nature as if they were independent of, or even separate from, His Power. * * * Nothing is more remarkable in the present state of physical research than what may be called the transcendental character of its results. And what is transcendentalism but the tendency to trace up all things to the relation in which they stand to abstract ideas? And what is this but to bring all physical phenomena nearer and nearer into relation with the phenomena of mind? The old speculations of philosophy which cut the ground from materialism by showing how little we know of matter, are now being daily reinforced by the subtle analysis of the physiologist, the chemist, and the electrician. Under that analysis matter dissolves and disappears, surviving only as the phenomena of Force; which again is seen converging along all its lines to some common centre—sloping through darkness up to God." * * * Creation by Law—Evolution by Law—

---

been, which has been, or the half equal to the whole, or give finite beings infinite attributes, which is the same thing. Limited intelligence therefore must be always liable to error, and we cannot conceive of a more effectual check to error than pain.

Development by Law, or as including all these kindred ideas, the Reign of Law, is nothing but the Reign of Creative Force, directed by Creative Knowledge, worked under the control of Creative Power, and in fulfilment of Creative Purpose."

Mr. R. S. Wyld, in a paper read before the Royal Society of Edinburgh, says, " Recent discoveries have established that heat is mechanical force, the two being mutually convertible without loss. The attraction of gravity and chemical attractions and repulsions are all the same physical force, and the entire external world is nothing but a manifestation of it,—a simple and grand conception, and one which enters alike the domain of physics, of speculative philosophy, and of theology, and which in all of these sciences is equally important. It represents the external world and its Creator as possessed of one immaterial and *spiritual* essence—power and intelligence being the attributes of the Creator, and *power subordinate and sustained the characteristic of the Creation.*" *

Bishop Berkeley holds that Deity inspires or causes the various mental sensations, and that there is no external world; Mr. Wyld that there is no such thing as matter, but that the world is a manifestation of Divine power—exhibited in space—so that the outer world has a real existence. For myself, I am not able to see how it is possible to separate the power of God from God himself; this conception may suit the exigencies of an ethical creed not based on Law, but as mind and matter are only the phenomenal modifications of the same common substance, so God and the power of God are equally inseparable, and I know nothing of *power subordinate and sustained* as something

* On the World as a Dynamical and Immaterial World.—*Proceedings of the Royal Society of Edinburgh*, vol. v., 1864-5. No. 67, p. 387.

separate from the Creator Himself. I can arrive at no other
conclusion but that God and Nature — the Creator and the
Creation — are One and Indivisible.

And need we fear to accept this conclusion? If we have
God manifest in the flesh, surely the Universe in its Unity
and Beauty is a not less worthy representation of the Absolute.
"All we see is but the vesture of God, and what we call laws
of Nature are attributes of Deity."* We feel that:—

> "The awful shadow of some unseen Power
> Floats tho' unseen among us." — *Shelley.*

> "And I have felt
> A presence that disturbs me with the joy
> Of elevated thoughts; a sense sublime
> Of something far more deeply interfused,
> Whose dwelling is the light of setting suns,
> And the round ocean, and the living air,
> And the blue sky, and in the mind of man;
> A motion and a spirit that impels
> All thinking things, all objects of all thought,
> And rolls through all things." — *Wordsworth.*

> "There lives and works
> A soul in all things, and that soul is God." — *Cowper.*

> "Earth, ocean, air, beloved brotherhood!
> If our great Mother have imbued my soul
> With aught of natural piety to feel
> Your love, and recompense the boon with mine;
> If dewy morn, and odorous noon, and even,
> With sunset and its gorgeous ministers,
> And solemn midnight's tingling silentness;
> If autumn's hollow sighs in the sere wood,
> And winter robing with pure snow and crowns
> Of starry ice the grey grass and bare boughs

---

* Philosophy of Necessity, p. 445.

Of spring's voluptuous pantings when she breathes
Her first sweet kisses, have been dear to me;
no bright bird, insect, or gentle beast,
I consciously have injured, but still loved
And cherished these my kindred;—then forgive
This boast, beloved brethren, and withdraw
No portion of your wonted favour now!"—*Shelley.*

"Neither is it only to the Old Pantheism, and nothing more, that we have been destined to return after all; but surely to something much higher:—something higher, in degree at least, if not in kind, than that to which the purest wisdom of antiquity was able to attain. For the self-knowledge which we may now say that our whole of Nature has gained of itself, is that it is the farthest possible from being entitled to claim absolutely for itself the proud name of the *Whole of Things!*— That is to say, the utmost that man is enabled to embrace even in his vaguest conceptions, is immeasurably inferior to the actual *tò pân*. Outside and beyond that which is the Whole *to us*, is always the unknown and unknowable that belongs to God only. The clear separation of the ideas,—the Whole that is our's, and the Whole that is *not* our's, but that includes our's as a part,—is our great gain over those highest minds of antiquity that may still have been dimly conscious of it. That Deity which was the Pan in the highest form to the philosophic world in general, has become to us subordinate to the still higher conception of the Divine Mystery that never can be unveiled to men.

"And the lower domain of Pantheism,—that which we call *lower* because it is accessible, though to them it was the *higher* because they had yet no means of estimating the degrees of remoteness:—this present belief which has come again to agree with that of Old, in recognizing that through the entirety of the Universe exists the whole of Deity that we can either know or conceive,—has at the same time the advantage over it, by all that the ages of experience have added. It is a Pantheism which contains within itself the rich contents of all the Religions and all the Philosophies the world has hitherto possessed; and yet farther, having the power now seen to be contained in it, the blessed necessity, of going on to make more and better!—Say we are returned to a parallel condition with that of the world in the time of Xenophanes;—what is there other than reason for rejoicing if we have also before us, in prophetic anticipation, a parallel repetition to be undergone, on a higher stage, of that succession of reigning mythologies whose early phase has imprinted so much of permanent delight in 'immortal song'!—Nay, is it not actual experience, and of a lovely sort, That instantly the mind recurs to the recognition of this Religion of Universal Nature, it seems instinctively to feel the living return of all the '*Lieblicher Geschlechts*' of the '*Götter Griechenlands!*'—Schiller was false to those inner breathings of true and present Deity which were the soul of his poetry, when he could lament for the '*entgötterte Natur!*' The old cry of the elder deities, the dispossessed genii of mountain, stream, and wood, that sent forth their plaintive wail when the triumphant personality of the lord of creation asserted itself in its first engrossing egoism:—the cry which the followers of the newly-incarnate Christ exalted in as the woe of departing demons, when it mourned 'Al, the great Pan is dead!'—comes back to our ears with a sense of beauty altogether new, now that we are no longer obliged to pervert its music by transposing it into the mythic representation of fact for which Christian Realism has taken it. Knowing, now, that the great Pan is *not* dead, and can never die;—and seeing that what that Christian Realism took for fact was fancy, and that what it took for fancy was fact;—we listen to the far-subdued plaint as pouring itself from the genuine pang of ancient severed faith, torn from that which was truly substance of its substance:—a reverberating moan that has never hushed, sighing along the ages, a night-wind through primæval pines, until its exquisite discord in a minor key is now once more resolving itself into the full harmony of an universal religion!

"And attuned to the spirit of religion such as this, has it not been always that a Wordsworth, an Emerson, and every true poet-nature has loved to stroll back into the world's early pastime, and see, forgetting all its store of grown-up acquisitions, 'what wisdom to the berries went'; silencing with 'pleasant fancies' the over-inquisitive self-ism that asks

'What influence me preferred
Elect to dreams thus beautiful?'

Ungratefully-contemned Nature!—what happy return of innocent child-like truth,—the lovely opposite of childish conceit,—is it to feel how far superior is her own naturalness to that which we had esteemed *super-natural*, only because we were slow to believe how much greater Nature could be in herself than that which we had imagined! In this sense, truly farthest from us be the notion of passing out of the range of the supernatural, and sitting down contented with the mere actual and present!—Only, into our heaven, not alone the 'faithful dog', but this little daisy, budding into spring-life, must bear us company!"— "Thoughts in aid of Faith," by *Sara S. Hennell.*

CHAPTER IV.

SPECULATIONS ON SPIRITUALISM AND OTHER ABNORMAL CONDITIONS OF MIND.

"The perfect observer in any department of science, will have his eyes as it were opened, that they may be struck at once by any occurrence, which, according to received theories ought not to happen, for these are the facts which serve as clues to new discoveries."—*Sir J. Herschel.*

"He who ventures to treat, *a priori*, a fact as absurd, wants prudence. He has not reflected on the numerous errors he would have committed in regard to many modern discoveries."—*Arago.*

"With regard to the miracle question, I can only say that the word 'impossible' is not to my mind applicable to matters of philosophy. That 'the possibilities of nature are infinite' is an aphorism with which I am wont to worry my friends. And if John Smith tells me to-morrow that by a word he can make a stone fall upwards, or cause the *Record* to speak with decency and fairness, or (say) the Bishop of Oxford, I may not think it worth while to go into the question, the value of John Smith's critical faculty being unknown to me, while the general course of experience is terribly against him, but I will not declare what he says to be *a priori* impossible. But if my friend Professor Tyndall should make either or both of the same assertions, I should feel bound at least to suspend my judgment until such time as the matter could be fully investigated."—*Professor Huxley.*

"In the last number of the *Spectator* (February 10, 1866), Professor Huxley has paid me the great compliment of stating that were I to tell him to-morrow that I could by a word cause a stone to fall upwards, he would feel bound to suspend his judgment until such time as the matter could be fully investigated. It is not often that I find myself unable to reciprocate the sentiments of my eminent friend. But on the present

70 SPECULATIONS ON SPIRITUALISM.

occasion I feel bound to say, that were he to confide to me the statement of his ability to reverse by a word the action of gravity, my judgment regarding him would find mournful expression in the line:—

'O what a noble mind is here o'erthrown.'"*

Professor Tyndall.

The Correlation of Force in Living Structures.

WHETHER the egg came before the chicken, or the chicken before the egg; whether organization depends upon life, or life upon organization, is still under dispute. What took place "In the beginning" it is difficult to say, but at the present time there seems to be a mutual dependence of organization upon life and life upon organization. Life—the vital spark, is, as far as we know, in all cases hereditary—for I hold the "spontaneous generation" theory to be at present "not proven." Life is transmitted from parent to offspring, and that offspring is dependent upon organization for the peculiar vital forces it displays; and with the organization perishes the life, at least in that form. As we have seen, however, the vital spark may lie dormant in

* It will be seen that I look upon Huxley's as by far the more philosophical position. We see a stone "fall upwards" when projected by a word or volition, or nervous force, from the arm. Now is it certain that mental force, a correlate of physical, can act upon the stone through no other medium but the nerves and muscles of the arm? Huxley says, "let me see it, that's all"; Tyndall says, "I won't look, the man's mad that asks me." Has gravitation then no correlate like the other forces? We find whole seas ascending from their basins, and descending again with a force sufficient to turn all the machinery in the world. In the following pages I wish it to be distinctly understood that personally I cannot vouch for the truth of what are called the spiritual manifestations; I have seen enough to induce me to believe they may be true, and the testimony of such men as Professor de Morgan, and many others equally honest, if not equally competent, I hold to be sufficient to warrant full investigation, and to "speculate" as I have done on their cause.

the seed for thousands of years until quickened into growth by heat and moisture; whether the same thing can take place in animals—as for instance in the toad said to be found alive in the red sandstone, is very problematical. Force, passing through the organization of the human body, accomplishes a great variety of work, according to the peculiarity of the structure through which it passes; and that which it does unconsciously through the stomach, liver, lungs, heart, circulation, muscles, &c., is quite as wonderful, and attended with quite as much intelligence as that which passes consciously through the brain. The perfection with which the different functions of the body are performed depends upon the condition of its organ. "The highest degree of organization giving the highest degree of thought." If the structure is impaired, disease takes place, and what is called the *vis medicatrix natura*, is probably nothing but the strong tendency that all vital structure has to assume its natural form or type.

The usual inlets to the mind for the forces without, are said to be the five senses of Sight, Hearing, Smell, Taste, and Feeling; but the whole body is an inlet to the mind, and we have besides a sense of temperature, of pleasure and pain, and a muscular sense.* The bat, and somnambules

---

* See "Man's Nature and Development," p. 97, et seq., by H. G. Atkinson, F.G.S., and Harriet Martineau. I consider this work the most valuable contribution towards Psychology based on Physiology which we have had since Gall and Spurzheim's works on Cerebral Physiology, or Phrenology. Professor Gregory, in the Preface to his work on Mesmerism says "The reader will find, in the work recently published by Mr. Atkinson and Miss Martineau, many striking facts connected with animal magnetism, which is one of the subjects treated of. Mr. Atkinson's observations on the functions of different parts of the brain as exhibited in the magnetic sleep are of the highest value, from that gentleman's great experience and intimate knowledge of the

and mesmerised people see without eyes; that is, the same force of light is conveyed to the brain through a different medium. Heat and electricity pervade the whole nervous system, and light, heat, and electricity, are but differing conditions of the same force or influence, and this seeing without eyes therefore may be accounted for. Dr. Howe, in his education of Laura Bridgman, showed how possible it was to reach the mind through other than its ordinary inlets. The sense of pleasure and pain must be distinguished from the feeling that attends the propensities and sentiments and other mental faculties and sensations. Mr. Atkinson, very properly, I think, gives them their separate organs in the brain. In accordance with this we find that as each organ can manifest only a limited amount of force according to its peculiar function, so only a certain amount of pain can at one time be endured. I know a lady who lately had eight teeth taken out at a sitting; after the first three she says she felt very little pain; and martyrs at the stake and criminals on the rack fortunately could only feel a limited amount of pain. Pain and Pleasure are transformed force—mental correlates; and Mr. Atkinson in mesmerising found that he could hold pain as it were, in the hollow of his hand; he could transfer it from another body to his own, and from one person to another, and "sleepers" who were so insensible that you might cut off their limbs without their knowledge, would feel instantly any pain inflicted on the mesmeriser.

---

subject. I should have made use of them but his work did not appear until the whole of the first part of mine was written." I have received several communications from Mr. Atkinson relating to the subjects of this work, while it has been going through the press, which I think are valuable, and which I have given in the Appendix.

Matter and Spirit the same in Essence.

As we have seen, external force, acting upon our peculiar organization, produces the phantom which we call the world: how, then, can spirit be *more ethereal* than this external force? or how can ghosts be more ghosts than what we call *gross material matter?* Spirits, therefore, if they exist, cannot be more ethereal; they may, however, be unseen, or we may be unconscious of their existence, because they may have no relation to our senses.

Time and Space.

That Time and Space are only "modes of thought," and can have no objective existence, or rather that the reality cannot accord with our conception, is evident from the fact that, according to our idea, the half of either Time or Space is as great as the whole; thus we have the infinite divisibility of atoms, and a past, as long as a future eternity.* We know

---

* Professor Tyndall tells us that, "Though we are compelled to think of space as unbounded, there is no mental necessity to compel us to think of it either as filled or as empty; whether it is filled or empty must be decided by experiment and observation." ("Constitution of the Universe."—*Fortnightly Review*.) Now this may be very true, still we must admit that the ground would take some time to get over: he, in fact must be a fast traveller who could go over infinite space in less than infinite time; particularly, if as the Professor tells us, the luminous ether—the interstellar medium, although infinitely more attenuated than any gas, has definite mechanical properties—those of a solid rather than a gas, "resembling jelly rather than air." We are told that we are by no means to consider this as a vague or fanciful conception on the part of scientific men, for that of its reality most of them are as convinced as they are of the existence of the sun and planets. Now although this "jelly" may be necessary to the exigencies of the vibratory theory with respect to light and heat, it must be evident that it renders the "observation" as to whether unbounded

only of thought, and of the force its correlate or equivalent; and can a thought be a mile long or a yard square? What,

---

space is filled or not, still more difficult. I do not think that the term infinite or boundless can be used in any other sense than as exceeding the bounds of our knowledge; whenever it is attempted to be used otherwise our first philosophers immediately fall into contradictions and absurdities. Righteousness, Holiness, Purity, Goodness, have only a relative existence, that is, can exist only in relation to finite things, how then can they be infinite? In fact Infinite Goodness and Infinite Wisdom are contradictions,—for goodness must be good to something, and knowledge must be of something, that is of some limited thing. Suppose there to have been a time when these things did not exist, these attributes could not have existed either. According to J. S. Mill there is no incorrectness of speech in the phrase Infinite Power—but in speaking of Knowledge, absolute is the proper word and not infinite. The highest degree of knowledge that can be spoken of with a meaning only amounts to knowing all that there is to be known: when that point is reached, knowledge has attained its utmost limit. So of goodness or justice: they cannot be more than perfect. To which the learned critic (Mansel I am told,) in the Contemporary Review replies, "Surely whatever Divine Power can do, Divine Knowledge can know as possible to be done. The one therefore must be as infinite as the other." Quite so, none of these attributes can be more than relative manifestations and therefore finite, for as the writer says, "Will Mr. Mill have the kindness to tell us what he means by goodness and knowledge 'out of all relation,' i. e., a goodness and knowledge related to no object on which they can be exercised; a goodness that is good to nothing, knowledge which knows nothing?" As attributes then must be finite, that is, can be exercised only in relation to finite objects, God is without attributes, that is, Pure Being. But that which has no attributes and nothing, to finite capacity is the same thing. The object then of the Hegelian Philosophy is to show how this nothing could become something; nothing however meaning not non-existence, but existence independent of sense or phenomena. "Being underlies all modes or forms of being." God creates, that is, Being becomes, and the fundamental principle of Hegelism is said to be "That God awoke to consciousness, and acquired a will, in the consciousness and will of man."

But "what can we reason, but from what we know" on this or on any other subject. And what do we know? Perhaps as much as

then, is distance? and can it apply to thought and feeling, that is, to what we call spirit? and need there be space, therefore, necessarily separating mind from mind?

The Correlation of the Vital and Mental Forces.

We are told, on what I believe to be good authority, that:—"Generally speaking, the average amount of daily

---

this:—the world was without form and void, that is nebulous, and as the force or heat concentrated, it gradually took first the inorganic and then the special living forms that now lie deep buried in the earth's crust, and with each stratum or layer, was a fresh correlation of mind or sentiency—an evolution, which covering the whole earth with a network of nerves, and passing again and again through different forms was refined and spiritualised till after countless ages it culminated in man, and "God became conscious in Humanity." But with respect to man, the highest intelligence here:—

> "Think you this mould of hopes and fears
> Could find no statelier than his peers
> In yonder hundred million spheres?
>
> This truth within thy mind rehearse,
> That in a boundless universe
> Is boundless better, boundless worse."—*Tennyson.*

> "Go to! You know not this nor that;
> Man has no measuring rod
> For Nature, Force, and Law, and what
> The best of men call God.
>
> For law, and life, and all the course
> Of lovely, shifting Nature,
> Are but the play of one wise Force,
> Which Moses called Creator.
>
> Think on your knees: 'tis better so,
> Than without wings to soar;
> What sharp-eyed Logic thinks to know
> We find when we adore.
>   "*J. S. B.*

"College, Edinburgh."

food necessary for healthy men is estimated at twelve ounces of beef, twenty ounces of bread, with about half-an-ounce of butter. These articles contain a force capable, if applied by a machine, of raising fourteen million pounds weight to a height of one foot; that is, the oxidation of the elements contained in them would give rise to an amount of heat equivalent to that effect. But in the human body, though it far surpasses all machines, in economy of force, the utmost amount of power attainable from them is not more than equivalent to three-and-a-half millions of pounds raised to the height of a foot; and an average day's labour does not exceed two millions of pounds thus raised. The difference is mainly due, doubtless, to the number of internal actions which are carried on in the living body; such as the circulation, the movements of respiration, and the production of animal heat. These consume a great part of the force of the food, and leave only a remainder to be disposed of in muscular exertion." *

Of course there must be great difference of opinion, not only as to the *amount* of force generated by the food, but also as to the mode of its expenditure. Thus we have Dr. Carpenter, supported by Helmholtz and Joule, differing from Professor Playfair, and the Professor differing from the above writer in the *Cornhill*, and we are prepared to receive the latter statement, therefore, only as a very wide approximation. But the question is, since force is indestructible, how is this force—immense in every estimate—expended? It will be found, I think, that thinking and feeling absorb a larger portion than the vital powers, and the vital than the merely muscular. In a notice of Dr. Playfair's book on "Food and Work," in the *Reader* of June 8, 1805, the writer says with

* *Cornhill Magazine*, September, 1861.

reference to the distribution of this force:—"In the steam-engine there are only two forces to be considered, the mechanical and the thermal. In man's body there are many different forces, but the study of them is rendered in one sense easy, and in another difficult, by the fact that, however varied they may be within the economy, they pass away into the external world in two phases only, the same phases in which they leave the steam-engine—viz., heat and movement. We speak of mental or cerebral force, of plastic or organic force, we look in upon the forces that go whirling round in our bodies, threading a devious path amid countless changes, working through most intricate machinery; but there are only two ways in which their effects can be measured by one standing without. They either produce muscular movements, or increase the temperature of the body. Intense mental effort cannot by itself be measured by the physiologist. The slight muscular movements through which it strives to express itself, are in no way to be thought of as gauging its intensity. Its only true measure is the amount of heat produced by that combustion of cerebral tissue, which is the condition of its development. So, also, the true measure of the force concerned in the fashioning of a hand, or of any other piece of wonderful organic work, is that heat which is the outcome of all the molecular processes busied therein. We may, if we like, divide the work of the body into various kinds. We may speak of the *opus mechanicum*, the muscular labour or useful work; of the *opus mentale*, or brain work; of the *opus mechanicum internum*, or inner muscular work, such as the heart's beat, the breath's play, the intestinal roll, and the arterial grasp; of the *opus vitale*, or chemical and fashioning work; of the *opus calorificum*, or the labour of keeping the body warm. Yet all these issue from the body as two kinds of work only, the *opus mechanicum*, the amount of foot-pounds a man can lift in a hard day's work, and the *opus calorificum*, the quantity of ice his body will cause to melt during the same time."

I believe this will prove to be a very inadequate account of the way in which the force received into the body again passes from it. The body is a system of solidified gases, or concentrated forces, (for particulars, see them as bottled up separately at the Kensington Museum,) in constant flux—influx and efflux—with everything around. No mention is here made of the electricity which is constantly flowing from the body in quantities more or less, as the nervous or other temperaments predominate in its structure. Nothing is said of the Odyle, to Reichenbach's sensitives visibly streaming from the extremities, and other parts of the body; or of the nervous force, composed perhaps of both the above, and which constitutes the peculiar strength of the magnetiser.

But the most elaborate apparatus in the body is that for the production of mental force. Here no doubt is the expenditure of the greater part of the fourteen million pounds lifting force that enters through the food, and the great question is what becomes of it? The writer above truly says, "Intense mental effort cannot by itself be measured by the physiologist," and yet in this direction lies the future course of a psychology based on physiology. And also Herbert Spencer—"Those modes of the unknowable which we call motion, heat, light, chemical affinity, &c., are alike transformable into each other, and into those modes of the unknowable which we distinguish as sensation, emotion, thought: these, in their turns, being directly or indirectly re-transformable into the original shapes." Exactly, "re-transformable!"—but when, where, and how? What becomes of every thought, as it is turned out of its "form" or mould in the brain? We know it is the exact equivalent of the physical force expended in producing it, and sometimes, to our cost, if we make a man angry, we get its exact equivalent in physical force again: but where it takes the form of muscular motion or of heat, is, I think, the exception, not the rule. Many facts now point to an atmosphere, or reservoir of thought, the result of cerebration, into which the thought and feeling generated by the brain is continuously passing. The brains and nervous systems of the whole sensitive existence are increasing and intensifying this mental atmosphere. The question is, does force exist more commonly as physical force or as mental? Does thought passing from us become free thought, or does it join some odylic or other medium? and does each separate thought retain its identity, that is, the form impressed upon it by our organization; or does it change its form, lose its consciousness, and thus no longer be thought and feeling? The Manifestationists, we are told by Professor Masson, hold the doctrine, "which, if developed, would assert nothing less than the phenomenal recoverability within the Cosmos of all sentiency that had ever belonged to it."* It is the general belief that force cannot exist by itself, but must belong to something else—must be the force *of* something; but I think I have previously shown that this belief is untenable. Bacon says: —"The magnetic or attractive energy allows of interposed media without destruction, and, be the medium what it may, the energy is not impeded. But if that energy or action has nothing to do with the interposed body, it follows that there is, at an actual time and in an actual place, an energy or natural action subsisting without body; since it subsists neither in the terminal nor in the intermediate bodies. Wherefore magnetic action may serve as an Instance of Divorce in relation to corporeal nature and natural action.

* Recent British Philosophy, p. 297.

To this may be added, by way of corollary, the following important result: that a proof thus be had, even by the mere philosopher of sense, of the existence of separate and incorporeal entities and substances. For if natural energy and action emanating from a body can exist, at a time and in a place, entirely without body, it is pretty clear that it may originally emanate from an incorporeal substance. For a corporeal nature seems just as much required for supporting and conveying as for exciting or generating natural action."*

We have no difficulty in conceiving of electricity as existing freely throughout space; but thought or mind, and electricity, are the same force in different forms or modes of manifestation. Electricity, although apparently in existence everywhere, only manifests itself to us through some kind of machine or body, so free thought can only manifest itself to us through some kind of organization. We know that physical force everywhere is in direct communication; that the remotest star is influencing our earth and our earth it; that every centre of force or body is acting upon every other body. It is not less so in the force which we call mind. Mind is in connection with all other mind.

There are certain individuals and nomadic tribes, in whom the vital system so predominates and the vital powers are so strong that they may literally be cut in two—lose legs and arms and life not be destroyed; and there are others in whom the nervous system so predominates that thought and feeling are generated so rapidly and in such quantities that there is no time for their re-correlation or re-transformation through the bodily organization, and they flow over into the general reservoir of mind. Nervous force may also be made to overflow into other bodily systems. To

---

* Novum Organon, Lib. xi., Aph. 57.

what extent, and in what way conscious thought and feeling, nervous force, electricity, and odyle, differ from each other or are necessary to each other, has not, I think, been correctly determined.

The interesting experiments of Dubois Raymond demonstrate the difference between nervous force and electricity, but Matteucci shewed that nervous force is capable of being transformed into electricity, under the influence of a peculiar structure, as illustrated in electrical fishes. Raymond's instruments may correctly measure the rate of the current along the nerve, but such experiments only show forcibly how much requires to be done. It is a step only in the right direction. When our philosophers, like Tyndall, pay the same attention to vital and mental forces as they now do to physical, we may hope to advance rapidly.

I know that it is the general belief, even of the spiritualists, that mind cannot exist apart from organization, but if force can exist apart from body, mind, which is only another form of force, may do so also. Thought and feeling are transformed force and cannot cease to exist, and the question is when it passes from us, in what form does it exist? Does it retain consciousness, that is, remain thought and feeling? In sleep what becomes of it? There I think it takes another form and is added to the vital force, as I have said before; but under a slight pressure on the brain, or temporary stoppage of the action of the heart, what becomes of it then? It is impossible to say what mind may be out of the body, as nothing can be known to us but in its action upon us— that is relatively—mind therefore cannot be known to us but in connection with organization, that is, our own organization. Sentiency is known to us only in connection with the brain and nervous system, and consciousness is reflection upon this sentiency, and is known to us only in connection with the highest intelligence here,—that is, Man. That some kind of feeble sentiency attends the vitality of plants I think is very probable. We cannot go further down, for although every atom acts intelligently, that is, towards a given purpose, the consciousness is *of* it, not *in* it.

When I speak then of a "thought" atmosphere, a "mental" atmosphere, or a "general" mind, I mean either mind or sentiency, or that condition of force which immediately precedes mind or consciousness, and which must exist in the brain, when from a slight pressure upon it, consciousness ceases.

To the transference of nervous force, and even mental states with it, from one body to another, and to the union of individual mind with the mental atmosphere, are owing I think it will be found, all the varied phenomena of somnambulism, mesmerism, and clairvoyance, and of what is called spiritualism.

The Senses are considered to be the only inlets of the world without to the mind within, but they are also the regulators by which no more of the influx of the general mind is admitted than is good for our conduct and happiness in common life, in the sphere of duties in which we are placed. A Somnambule is enabled to do without the senses, and in a state of trance or mesmerism the barrier between individual and general mind seems partially broken down.

The Conditions attending Influx or Inspiration.

The bodily conditions requisite to induce this state seem to be that the "meddling senses" should be laid asleep, and that all other parts of the body should have as little to do as possible. Prayer and fasting and solitude are particularly efficacious to this end. In solitude the senses are quiet, and under long and continued fasting the vital system having little to do, becomes partially absorbed in the nervous, and prayer induces a concentration of mental action on subjects that have no direct connection with the body.

The bodily conditions we are considering predominate much more in some races than in others—in the Eastern and sunny, than in the Western and more Northerly. Among the Hindoos they are most prevalent. The Hindoos are much better subjects for mesmerism than Europeans, and the arts of Divination and Magic, which are based on this partial breaking down of the barrier between general and individual mind, have always been much more in practice. To be absorbed in universal Being is the great aim of the religious fanatic in India, and many succeed in becoming partially so, even in the body. "The one infallible diagnostic of Buddhism is a belief in the infinite capacity of the human intellect. * * * The idea of Deified man *is there;* but this loses itself in another, that there is in man, in humanity, a certain Divine Intelligence, which at different times and in different places manifests itself more or less completely." * * *. The natural eye takes account only of appearances; it requires the severest discipline for a man to behold the Reality. * * * Wisdom is viewed as wholly social and experimental in one; internal and mystical in the second; strangely mixed with what is superhuman and eternal in the third."*

The Buddhist Priest by the aid of irdhi is represented as being able to listen to all sounds, and know all thoughts, and see all former births, and watch the course of all transmigrations, and learn the cause of all causes. The next stage—the great desideratum, is, that having been subject to

* The Religions of the World and their Relation to Christianity, pp. 76, 85, 93, by Rev. F. D. Maurice.

birth, decay, sorrow, weeping, grief, discontent, and vexation—the consummation of the whole series of births and deaths is now attained, and that is, to pass again into "Nothingness." * This doctrine originated some 628 years before the Chiristian Era, and yet we might almost suppose that the doctrine of eternal torments had cast its shadow before.

Important news travels faster in India by Mental Telegraph than by the Electric Telegraph. The results of important battles have been known days before the intelligence could arrive by the ordinary or official means. The source of these tidings cannot be traced; the natives say "it is in the air," and there has often been a generally uneasy feeling pervading mens' minds preceding ill news, when nothing definite has been known.

The weakening of the vital force by disease, or partial paralysis, often intensifies the mind and sustains it in fuller action.

Bacon tells us that "when the mind is withdrawn and collected within itself, and not diffused into the organs of the body, is the state which is most susceptible of divine influxions."

In trance, and seeing in the crystal, and under hypnotism and mesmerism, "The mind is withdrawn and collected within itself, and not diffused into the organs of the body," and it is thus intensified, and the barriers between it and other minds, and between it and the general mind, are partially broken down. "The internal faculties appear to be loosened from the sense, and to receive impressions direct from without."†

---

* The Legends and Theories of the Buddhists, by R. Spencer Hardy.

† "Each sense faculty is adapted to receive the peculiar influence or impression to which it relates: but the instrumentality or intervention of the external sense does not seem always requisite. The internal

Of course any influx of mind can only act in and through the human faculties, and cannot overstep the limits of their power or function, that is, it can give no kind of knowledge

---

faculties seem to be loosened from the sense, and to receive impressions direct from without; to be open to conditions to which the senses were not fitted. It does not seem to be any strain upon reason to suppose this. Few can give any account of the process by which they came at many of their conclusions. *Clairvoyance* or prophecy is no greater step from our ordinary condition than seeing would be to a blind person, who would say, 'I could only take up Nature bit by bit before, and put them bits together, and then form but a very imperfect conception: but now I recognize all at once; the distant, as well as that which is near.' You set free the inner faculties, and open 'the eye of the mind' to the outward influences of a grosser sense; and knowledge flows in unobstructed. You are as one who was blind, but can now see. The new sense and the old are equally intelligible, and both inexplicable. You cannot explain a process where there is none. The imperfect sense, the blind have a process to explain: but in clear-seeing there is no process but the fact."—*Man's Nature and Development*, p. 276.

Mr. Atkinson also says, "I think it is worthy of remark what Bacon has suggested, that we might receive other and fuller information from external objects had we other senses fitted to receive the impressions, and I think this may be demonstrated to be true, and hence if the inner sense can be brought in relation to the whole truth by shutting up the ordinary sense media and by mesmeric action, &c., enabling such inner powers to be brought in direct contact with the entire fact, a deeper insight would be attained, as seems to be the case, and men acquire a more intuitive perception and clairvoyant character, under such irregular and abnormal conditions. And certainly things do become often, as it were, reversed under unusual conditions; a dog attaining the instinct to seek the medicine it requires when sick; the stem of a tree throwing out root, the root developing into flowers, and so on. The instances are innumerable and the laws of the normal action would be brought to light by such irregular actions and transformations under unusual conditions, just as the irregular or exceptional phenomena of the planets have given a knowledge of the laws of their motion—the rule proved in the exception."

which it is not their province to bestow. What is the limit of that power when the organs are very large or very much excited has by no means been determined. What is the power that enabled Sir Isaac Newton and George Bidder to make their algebraic, geometric, and arithmetical calculations, giving at a glance results that it took long to work out on paper? What peculiar constitution of the organ of Locality is it that guides the carrier pigeon on its homeward progress, or the blind seal that found its long way home, or dogs that have come home from abroad, without, as far as we know, consulting any of the finger posts? What is it in the more excitable brain of woman that enables her, on a first interview, often to read character correctly, and which in the larger organs of such men as Shakspeare and Scott has enabled them to read the natural language of the mind, and paint character so correctly without any principle or knowledge of mental Science? Again, we have the action of the organ of Wonder or Faith. The senses call the Perceptive faculties into action, and Wonder gives a sense of reality—a belief in the real objective existence of something corresponding to the ideas which they furnish. In the abnormal or greatly excited state of this organ, a reflex action takes place; Wonder itself calls the Perceptive faculties into play, and figures are produced which appear just as real as when the action on the Perceptives comes through the senses. Many ghosts may be accounted for in this way. The Æsthetic faculties also when isolated from worldly cares and passions or when naturally predominant, or unusually active or excited, seem to bring the mind into direct union with nature.

Heat and electricity are constantly passing off from the body; so is mind. We influence every one and every thing about us, and are influenced by them. We photograph our mental states on all the rooms we inhabit.* We have probably some organ that takes cognizance of such "emanations," and which places us *en rapport* with the general mind. What Mr. Atkinson calls the "Eye of the Mind" may exercise some such function.† This faculty is supposed to bear the same relation to the internal action of the mind, as the mind itself does to external objects or forces. It sees at a glance, and generalizes the action of all the mental faculties, and is therefore the highest of all our powers. As the Perceptive faculties, aided by the Senses, take cognizance of body or the action of physical forces, this takes cognizance of Spiritual or Mental forces. It is a sort of inner sense, through whose medium we may be put in communication with mind without ourselves as well as the mind within. This organ, if existing at all, which I think highly probable, seems but very partially

---

* A madman may be detected by the smell, and the diseased condition of his mind influences even healthy brains injuriously. With respect to bodily emanations we must remember that a bloodhound will follow a man over fifty or even one hundred miles of country—what would these emanations have been if confined to a single room! These emanations also have a distinctive character, for a dog seeking his master knows if he has been in a room although fifty other men may be there.

† "Beneath the central organ of Comparison, lying under Benevolence, is what has been termed by a somnambule the 'Eye of the Mind'. This seems to be the power of judgment:—we might call it the Intuitive faculty; for it is this which is chiefly concerned in clairvoyance. • • • This faculty, this mental eye, seems to receive the results of the doings of the other faculties, and to be, properly speaking, perhaps the mind sense, joining as it does with the Conscious power. Here seems to be the organ of the suggestive faculty of Genius. This seems to be the true Mind power, or Intellect. It seems to split off into the senses, as light divides off into colours, or sound into notes, but to contain within itself the power of mind concentrated, when cut off from the ordinary character of sense and reason. Then all time seems to become as one duration; space seems as nothing; all passions and desires become hushed; truth becomes an insight, or *through-sight;* and life a law."— *Man's Nature and Development,* p. 76. (See also Appendix A.)

developed in the bulk of mankind, and its action is altogether misconstrued in those in whom it is fully developed. In our blindness and ignorance we have but one term for such powers —"imagination—all imagination—overstrained imagination," &c., as we call the action of our higher feelings, sentimental. The ordinary habits and intercourse of the world, where all are absorbed in mere externals—ordinary sense and perception, and little carking cares and animal impulses, give but little chance for the growth and activity of such an inner sense, and it is not surprising that its promptings should be misunderstood and misinterpreted. Of course we can know only what our faculties tell us, and we can sympathize only with what we have feelings to sympathize with; our strongest feelings induce us to protect and take care of our own bodies; we have feelings also that make us a part of the body of Society; we have feelings that place us in relation to the beauties and harmony of Creation; and we have this faculty that places us in relation to the general mind or spirit. Mr. Atkinson says, Clairvoyants call it the "Eye of the Mind," Spiritualists call it "The Spiritual Eye," it is the principal source of Influx or Inspiration, and probably places us in the same relation to the Universal Spirit as our other faculties do to our fellow creatures.

By the general mind I mean the general mind of humanity, or perhaps I ought to say of the whole of sensitive existence, —for I have not seen evidence of any knowledge that can be said to be superhuman.

To say that force is everywhere connected, atom with atom, and world with world, is to say that mind, its correlate, is everywhere connected—is one and indivisible; but what we can see in the great mirror of mind when in union with it, remains to be investigated; so far as that investigation has proceeded, I think what we can see in no case exceeds the combined intellectual power of the whole human mind. Whatever has been, or is, in the human mind, or which our natural powers can reach, that we can see, and that only. What we can see cannot exceed the power of the instrument. The prescriptions by clairvoyants for the cure of disease in Mesmer's time were always in accordance with the fashionable modes of cure of that time; and Andrew Jackson Davis, and other Seers, although often reaching the highest rounds in philosophy, never go past what has been already known, or what human faculty can teach or comprehend. They can read the mind of the age, but they rarely if ever anticipate scientific discovery. They give us, as in Davis's case, what the *Edinburgh Review* (October, 1865), calls "a mad jumble of Spinozaism, Fourierism, Saint Simonianism, Swedenborgianism, and Rationalism," and although here may be found the most important psychological truths and the most advanced social science, yet there is so much nonsense mixed with sense that observation and experience is as much required to sift the true from the false in these revelations, as in any that come through the ordinary means of knowing. By union of mind with the general thought medium, and of mind with mind, that is seen which cannot be seen by the natural eye, both near and distant, time and space forming no impediments. *I have heard* a young girl, in the mesmeric state, minutely describe all that was seen by a person with whom she was *en rapport*, and in some cases more than was seen or could be seen, such as the initials in a watch which had not been opened, and also describe persons and scenes at a distance, which I afterwards discovered were correctly described, *beyond a possibility of doubt*. But Prevision! surely there are instances of prevision that are superhuman? Science enables us to anticipate the future; there is an established order of nature everywhere, and it is a correct calculation of cause and affect that enables us to prophesy. It is the organ of causality that takes cognizance of this invariable sequence, and we have only to suppose that organ from large size or excitement, to be as abnormal in its action and power of calculation as the organ of number often is in arithmetical calculation, and we might see very far into the future.* Perhaps one of the most singular and best authenticated cases of preternatural mental power is that related by Zschokke of himself, in his Autobiography, pp. 160, 172. He says, "It has happened to me, sometimes on my first meeting with strangers, as I listened silently to their discourse, that their former life, with many trifling circumstances therewith connected, or frequently some particular scene in that life, has passed quite involuntarily, and, as it were, dream-like, yet perfectly distinct before me. * * * For a long time I held such visions as delusions of the fancy, and the more so as they showed me even the dress and motions of the actors, rooms, furniture, and other accessories. * * * I myself had less confidence than any one in this mental jugglery. So often as I revealed my visionary gifts to any new person, I regularly expected to hear the answer: 'It was not so.' I felt a secret shudder when my auditors replied that it was true, or when their astonishment

* "It is, however, admitted that this foresight does not extend to the influence of external circumstances by which the ordinary course of the phenomena may be interrupted. Thus, a patient may predict that on a certain day and at a certain hour he may have an epileptic fit, but in the mean time he may be accidentally killed or intentionally murdered. His predictions of the phenomena of his own disease are to be understood in the same sense as the prediction of the astronomer of the rise and fall of the tides in a particular port, that is, subject to the implied condition, that the natural course of things shall not be deranged by any external and irregular disturbing cause."—*Monthly Chronicle*, vol. I., p. 298. It would thus seem, as I have said, that the prevision does not exceed the preternatural power of the organ of causality. (See also Appendix B.)

betrayed my accuracy before they spoke.   *   *   *   I shall
not say another word of this singular gift of vision, of which
I cannot say it was ever of the slightest service; it manifested
itself rarely, quite independently of my will, and several times
in reference to persons whom I cared little to look through.
Neither am I the only person in possession of this power."
He met, he tells us, with an old Tyrolese, who *for some time
after fixing his eyes upon him*, read him as he had read others.
What has been called Socrates's Demon was an intuition of a
similar kind, although quite different in its function, as by it
Socrates was repeatedly made acquainted with events about to
happen. He is said to have regarded it in very much the
same light as Zschokke did; he was, however, an implicit
believer in supernatural communications. We have previously
said that whatever has been, or is, in the human mind,
clairvoyants can recognize; but what should turn the attention and apparently confine the power to this one particular
direction? Here in Zschokke's case, was a mental individuality — the whole of a man's previous existence, presented
to him and retained in such perfect form that it could be
recognized by a separate and indifferent person, and had
its possessor not been still living, it might have been, and
no doubt would have been, claimed as the soul of the
departed "communicating."

What is Memory?

The consideration of the nature of memory may perhaps
help to throw some light upon this question. It is a
difficult subject this of Memory, of which we must not speak
too confidently, and cannot speak too modestly. All the
powers in nature could not make the acorn grow into anything
else than an oak. Yet what can we see or recognize in the

small, soft, apparently homogeneous germ in the acorn that can give it this power of action and resistance? Life, and the entire character and direction of that life, depend upon structure, so do the forms of thought, and any subject or object of attention and interest acting upon the brain, photographs itself there, that is, it slightly alters its structure; and fresh mental force passing over these "moulds," turns out similar thoughts and feelings to those that formed them. This it is, joined to certain powers of Association, or automatic action of the brain, by which thoughts and feelings are blended and made to follow each other in a definite order, which possibly constitutes memory. It is probably these old photographs which Zschokke's "Eye of the Mind," or other organ which gives "the intuition of character," as he himself seemed to suppose, could read. The youthful brain is the most easily impressible, and the memory becomes bad and retains few impressions as the brain ossifies and its plastic power decreases in age; that part going first which came the earliest into activity—the memory for names, &c. On the other hand there is a tendency in nature to rebuild the early structure—to produce the original type on which a particular kind of memory depended, and the memory of youth returns.

Mr. A. Bain makes memory to depend on "specific growth;" he says, "For every act of memory, every exercise of bodily aptitude, every habit, recollection, train of ideas, there is a specific grouping, or co-ordination, of sensations and movements, by virtue of specific growths in the cell junctions, and of separate nervous growths for each new and separate acquisition." *

* The Intellect viewed Physiologically.—*Fortnightly Review*, February 1, 1866.

SPIRITUALISM.

Genuineness of the Phenomena.

But is the above hypothesis, and the normal and abnormal condition of mind described, sufficient to account for the phenomena of Spiritualism? Of such phenomena as are genuine I think they are. But are any of the alleged facts genuine; are not fraud and superstition and self-delusion sufficient to account for them all? Although a great deal may be accounted for in this way still a large residue remains of most important psychological phenomena. The spiritualists have a theory to support, for the good, as they suppose, of all mankind; we must not be surprised therefore if the facts require a little forcing to fit that theory, and if the theorists often think they see what they so strongly wish to see. For most of the alleged facts we may readily find the testimony of twelve honest witnesses, and we must not reject that testimony, because in ignorance of mental science, and the bodily conditions upon which it depends, such facts are used to support superstitions which are vanishing before the advancing light of the age. The strength of intolerance and bigotry is generally in proportion to ignorance, but I do not think any candid person, after examination, can resist the testimony in favour of the facts themselves. The article in the *Cornhill Magazine*, "Stranger than Fiction," is rightly attributed I believe to Robert Bell, and Dr. Gully, of Malvern, says of it, " I can state with the greatest positiveness that the record made in that article is, in every particular correct," and "that no sleight-of-hand, or other artistic contrivance produced what we heard or beheld." So it may be presumed that Dr. Gully was present on this occasion, and as Mr. Home is stated in that account in the *Cornhill* to have floated about the room, over the heads of the persons present, witches riding about on broom-sticks may be "founded in fact" after all. The above statement of Dr. Gully's is to be found in "Incidents of my Life," by D. D. Home; of which book a "Friend" in the "Introductory Remarks," says, "whatever be the preconceptions of the reader regarding Mr. Home, he will scarcely fail after reading this volume, to acknowledge that the author writes as a man thoroughly in earnest, and who has himself no doubt of the phenomena that attend him." In this I most heartily concur; still Mr. Home may not be altogether free from the unconscious effort to make facts square to his theory, or, when "the spirits", on some important occasion, were not sufficiently demonstrative, from giving to them some little assistance.

Mr. T. Adolphus Trollope, writing from Florence to the *Athenæum*, March 21, 1868, says, "I have been present at very many 'sittings' of Mr. Home in England, many in my own house in Florence, some in the house of a friend in Florence. * * * I have seen and felt physical facts wholly and utterly inexplicable, as I believe, by any known and generally received physical laws. I unhesitatingly reject the theory which considers such facts to be produced by means familiar to the best professors of legerdemain. I have witnessed also very surprising and extraordinary metaphysical manifestations. But I cannot say that any of these have been such as wholly to exclude the possibility of their being deceptive,—and indeed, to use the honest word required by the circumstances, fraudulent.

"This is my testimony reduced to its briefest possible expression.

"If it be asked what impression, on the whole, has been left on my mind by all that I have witnessed in this matter, I answer, one of perplexed doubt, shaping itself into only one conviction that deserves the name of an opinion, namely, that quite sufficient cause has been shown to demand further patient and careful inquiry from those who have the opportunity and the qualifications needed for prosecuting it; that the facts alleged and the number and character of the persons testifying to them are such that real seekers for truth cannot satisfy themselves by merely pooh-poohing them."

But the testimony most to be relied on for the reality of the phenomena is that of perhaps one of the most acute and hard-headed philosophers of this day, not a spiritualist but a Professor of Mathematics, Augustus de Morgan. In the admirable Preface to Mrs. de Morgan's book, "From Matter to Spirit", he says "I am perfectly convinced that I have both seen and heard, in a manner which would make unbelief impossible, things *called* spiritual which cannot be taken by a rational being to be capable of explanation by imposture, coincidence or mistake." He says "there has been a sudden and general recognition of the existence of phenomena which historical enquiry shows never to have been entirely unknown." The base of the spiritualist hypothesis he tells us is "that some intelligence, which is not that of any human beings clothed in flesh and blood, has a direct share in the phenomena." And again, "My state of mind which refers the whole either to unseen intelligence, or something which man has never had any conception of, proves me to be out of the pale of the Royal Society," (p. 27,) but, he says, "if these things be spirits, they show that pretenders, coxcombs, and liars are to found on the other side of the grave as well as on this."—(p. 44.) "When it comes to what is the cause of these phenomena, I find I cannot adopt any explanation which has yet been suggested. If I were bound to choose among things that I can conceive, I should say that there is some sort of action of some combination of will, intellect, and physical power, which is not that of any of the human beings present. But thinking it very likely that the universe may contain a few agencies—say half-a-million—about which no man knows anything, I cannot but suspect that a small proportion of these agencies—say five thousand—may be severally competent to the production of all the phenomena, or may be quite up to the task among them. The physical explanations which I have seen are easy, but miserably insufficient; the spiritual hypothesis is sufficient, but ponderously difficult." Of the possible existence of such occult forces Mr. W. R. Grove, writing however not on Spiritualism, but on Light, says, "The conviction that every transient gleam (of light) leaves its permanent impress on the world's history, also leaves the mind to ponder over the many possible agencies of which we of the present day may be as ignorant as the ancients were of the chemical character of light."*

Dr. Ashburner tells us (quoted in "An Exposition of Spiritualism," p. 290), that "A force which is a material agent, attended by or constituting a coloured light, emanates from the brain of man, when he thinks—that his will can direct its impingement—and that it is a motive power." †
Mr. Atkinson also, in the same work, (p. 205,) says, "The so called spiritual manifestations arise from a force projected and directed by the unconscious sphere of the mind or soul"; and before the occurrence of such manifestations he

* Correlation of Physical Force, p. 159.
† The Catholics tell us that the heads and countenances of Saints in their Church have shone out with a glorious brightness, as the face of an angel. No doubt the "auriole" was the odylic light of Reichenbach, or this coloured light of Dr. Ashburner, much more evident, even to "sensitives", in some persons than in others.

remarked, (Letters, p. 114,) "amongst matter to be inquired into are all cases of persons who cast off an influence which causes motion in surrounding objects," &c.*

Mr. D. D. Home's explanation is, "That the spirits accomplish what they do through our life-sphere, or atmosphere, which was permeated by our wills; and if the will was contrary the sphere was unfit for being acted upon," † consequently scepticism marred the forces at work. He tells us "One of his friends was converted from previous unbelief, by seeing a female hand, which was visible to all in the room, slowly forming in the air a few inches above the table, until it assumed all the apparent materiality of a real hand, (p. 182); but he tells us, spirits have great difficulty in presenting, and thus incarnating these hands out of the vital atmosphere of those present, and that their work was spoilt, and had to be recommenced, when they were interfered with."—(p. 77.)

We are also told in "Incidents in my Life," that Dr. Carpenter "thinks these phenomena are produced by 'unconscious cerebration,'" and Mr. J. D. Morell refers them to "reflex action of the mind"; we may presume, therefore, that both these gentlemen accept the genuineness of the phenomena,—and their explanation, taken jointly, with Dr. Ashburner's, does not much differ, probably, from my own, although they

* "Every fragment or material we can hold or see is a storehouse of force. In the case of certain compounds like gunpowder, we know how to unlock chemical forces of affinity and cohesion, and to obtain by a sudden expansion and re-arrangement of atoms, a mechanical power that rends the rock or propels the ball; but it is startling to think that the most quietly-behaved bodies we find on the globe, the granite frames of mountains, or the very dust particles on the road, are like sleeping lions, full of potential force, which they can give out the moment the balance of their affinities are disturbed."—"Physical Forces."—*The Intellectual Observer*, April, 1866.

† Incidents of my Life, p. 75.

might repudiate it. What I have called a mental or thought atmosphere is the result of cerebration, and as far as we know it is devoid of consciousness, until it becomes so as "reflected" in our own organizations. Conscious cerebration, or mind, as we have seen, is transformed force, received into the body in the food, and is, like all force, persistent or indestructible, and when it passes from us, it probably becomes unconscious cerebration, and joins other force of the same nature, and through its medium all brains are brought into union, so that what one brain is conscious of another may be, and what is in the mind of sentiency becomes common property. This "unconscious cerebration," the produce of the whole of sentient existence, may again become sentiency in animals and consciousness in man, and thus we have so much as is true in the doctrine of transmigration of souls. The light of the soul beams brightly for a time in our consciousness, but the rays although scattered never cease to exist, but form a gradually intensifying atmosphere of their own. As the individual constituents of our bodies take new forms, so no one particle of mind is lost.

Application of the Theory: Physical Force, Table Moving, Rapping, Levitation, &c.

Now let us see how the facts of Spiritualism accord with our Theory. Mrs. de Morgan's record of those facts in "From Matter to Spirit," is on the whole fair, and even philosophical, when not encumbered by old superstitions and an anthropological theology.

We have to account for physical force and intelligence supposed to be not that of any human beings present. With respect to physical force, gravitation and nervous force or "unconscious cerebration," are correlates, that is, transformable, like heat and electricity, into each other, and, like heat and electricity, although quantitatively the same, they are qualitatively different, that is, they differ in their mode of action, and when a table becomes charged with the nervous force it seems to dispossess or change the character of gravitation, and it acts *less* as a downward attraction. The rising and moving of tables and other articles of furniture exactly accords in the mode of action with this loss of gravitation or weight. When intelligence appears, and this nervous force or "cerebration" acts more or less consciously under the power of the Will, we are told in the history of " Mary Jane"*, that the physical force ceases; as in the *animal* body it is changed in its form of manifestation. I say, more or less consciously, because the rapping is sometimes the effect of conscious but more often of unconscious cerebration. As an illustration of the conscious, Mrs. de Morgan says, "As each rap seemed to be shot through my arm, it was accompanied by a feeling like a slight blow or shock of electricity, and an aching pain," &c. "This experiment," she says, "seemed to prove that the nerves of the human body were necessary, if not for the production, at least for the propagation of the sounds." † Her maid Jane described the effect produced, as "first a throbbing, then a creaking, then a full-formed sound like a concussion of air, which she said passed through her arms like an electric shock" (p. 21.) I have not seen much of these phenomena, but what I once saw by a celebrated medium was of this character: he took my umbrella and held it at arm's length against the looking glass and the door and other things, and got three distinct throbbing pulsations, but he could not do

---

* Mary Jane; or Spiritualism Chemically Explained.
† From Matter to Spirit, p. 17.

the same with his own small stick till a gentleman took hold of his other hand. That the raps were always three, neither more nor less, showed, I inferred, that they were to some extent under the control of the will. That these raps are subjective, and not made by spirits, I think is evidenced by their attending only upon some people, and those of peculiar constitution, and that those people, as in Mr. Home's case, sometimes lose the power, and that for months together. The author of " Spiritualism Chemically Explained," says, " But now a further progressive phase took place; it was not necessary to sit at the table; if my wife lay on the sofa, the responsive taps would come apparently from behind the sofa; and even in bed, the conversation was carried on by Mary Jane, (the name he gave to the supposed cause of or instrument in these manifestations, as he did not believe in 'the spirits,') either by raps over our heads, or apparently on a chest of drawers close by the bed. One night, after we were in bed, I was talking with Mary Jane, and I perceived that my wife was getting sleepy, and it entered my mind to test whether the emanations continued during sleep, so I continued the conversation. By degrees, the responses became slower and fainter, and by the time I was convinced that my wife was fast asleep, they ceased altogether."—(p. 810.) Generally Mary Jane would rap anywhere she was asked to do.— (p. 819.) During his wife's illness, from whom he supposed Mary Jane to be an Odylic emanation, the manifestations were very feeble.—(p. 828.)

When we consider the power generated by the food in the body,—a power equal to raising fourteen millions of pounds one foot, the consumption of not half of which is at present accounted for; and considering the great number of purposes to which this power is applied, and the different forms it takes in the human body, we ought not to feel surprised

that individuals should possess this power of rapping. When
we throw a stone the motion is owing to force derived from our
bodies, which force is again given out as heat when the motion
ceases,—the arm is merely the leverage by which the force
is used. Why may not force be used, projected as this is
by the Will, without such leverage? We are accustomed
to a visible and tangible medium, and we confound this mere
medium with the force itself. Professor Tyndall, in a correspondence on Science and Prayer, in the *Pall Mall Gazette*,
(October, 1865,) says, "The external motion of your arm
is derived immediately from a motion *within* your arm,—it
is in fact this motion in another shape. While you were
pushing your inkstand a certain amount of oxidation occurred
in the muscles of your arm, which oxidation, under normal
circumstances, produces a certain definite amount of heat.
To move the inkstand, a certain quantity of that heat has
been consumed which is the exact amount of the work done.
You could do the same work with the same amount of heat
from an ordinary fire. The force employed is the force of
your food which is stored up in your muscles. The motor
nerves pull the trigger and discharge the force. You have
here a series of transformations of purely physical energy,
with one critical point involved in the question, "what causes
the motor nerves to pull the trigger? Is the cause physical
or super-physical? Is it a sound or a gleam, or an external
prick or purpose, or some internal uneasiness that stimulates
the nerves to unlock the muscular force—or is it free will?"
There can, I think, be no doubt as to the source of the force
causing the rapping—the body lets off a series of percussion caps, it does not discharge the whole machine, and the
question is through what medium out of the body this is
effected, and what pulls the trigger? for it is evident that the
rapping is not always voluntary, or under the control of

the will. Mr. Home declares that the manifestations that attend upon him are quite without his own control. They are sometimes voluntary, however, as Mary Jane would rap whenever she was asked,—and the power of the will, inside the body as well as outside, has yet to be ascertained. The *Spectator*, in the article we have already quoted, "Science and Miracle," says " almost every physiologist will admit the power which pure Will has over the nervous system,—that it can prolong consciousness and even life itself for certain short spaces, by the mere exertion of vehement purpose. Physicians tell you constantly that such and such a patient may no doubt, if it be sufficiently important, by a great effort command his mind sufficiently to settle his affairs, but that it will be at the expense of his animal force,—in short, that it will be a *free transfer of force* from the digestive and so to say vegetating part of his system, to that part of his physical constitution, his nervous system, which lies closest, as it were, to the will, (and which in fact is changed in form and becomes will). Nay, we have heard physicians say that patients, by a great effort of pure will, have, as they believe prolonged their own lives for a small space, that is, have imparted we suppose, through the excitement produced by the will on the nervous system and so downwards, a certain slight increase of capacity to assimilate food to the failing organic powers of the body. In other words, we conclude, just as the organism is failing to draw supplies of physical force from the outward world, its power of doing so may be slightly prolonged,—the outward world drained of a small amount of force it would otherwise have kept in stock, and the organism compelled to absorb it—by a pure volition. Can there be a clearer case of action of the supernatural on the natural, even granting that the sum total of physical force is not altered, but only its application changed?" No doubt the will has all the power that physicians thus ascribe to it and more, but there is nothing in such power supernatural, as the *Spectator* supposes. "A pure volition" is the correlate or equivalent of so much physical force, and this change of vital or vegetative force to mental, and of mental back to vital, is seen to be one of the commonest facts in nature when once observed. There is always a sufficient mental force in reserve, if the will be strong enough to bring it into action, to act upon the vital, that is, the digestive and assimilative powers, and thus to gain new force for a time from the world without.

Intelligence.

Besides the "levitation" and rappings, the Spiritualist hypothesis assumes "the co-operation of an Intelligence which is not that of any human being," and Professor de Morgan's state of mind he says "refers the whole either to unseen intelligence or to something which man has never had any conception of." My own opinion is that there is an emanation from all brains, the result of both conscious and unconscious cerebration, forming, not spirits, but a mental or spiritual atmosphere, by means of which peculiar constitutions —mediums and others, are put *en rapport* with other brains or minds, so as to become conscious of whatever is going on there. I believe the intelligence which manifests itself in a "circle," which is not that of any person present, or as Mrs. de Morgan expresses it, "the elementary idea or truth sought to be conveyed, and which does not originate with the medium," is the simple result, upon an enlarged and more general state, of that "thought reading" which we see every day in clairvoyants. This spiritual atmosphere is also able to bring the mind into immediate contact, without the aid of the senses, with whatever it pervades, so that people can see both near and distant what they could not see with ordinary eyesight. This is only another well known phase of Clairvoyance. Indeed Mrs. de Morgan tells us "that every wonderful effect produced by mesmerism has since found its explanation or its counterpart in spiritual phenomena." — (p. 49.) Again she says "It is indisputable that the medium is under mesmeric influence, but *what is that* influence? and in these cases whence does it proceed?"

To what extent, and under what conditions, through this atmosphere of cerebration, mind can act on mind, can only be matter of observation and experiment.

First we have to consider the conditions under which we can be put into contact or communication with this "atmosphere." The bodily constitutions requisite seem greatly to vary both in power and the mode of manifestation, and among what are called "mediums" there seems to be a power of both efflux and afflux, as we have the mesmeriser and the mesmerised—the giver and receiver. Some mediums have the power of intensifying the spiritual atmosphere, others of receiving whatever this atmosphere may contain. "Great exercise of mediumship," Mrs. de Morgan tells us, "is likely to exhaust the more delicate constitution of the nervous sanguine, (p. 4,) while great activity in the brains of those concerned interferes with the experiment," (p. 0,) the one state referring to the first class of mediums, the other to the latter. "The unseen power," we are told, "prefers a passive state to a positive action of the brain," (p. 89,) and our own force requires to be exhausted by physical effort, by illness, by watching, fasting, or prayer, before we can become the recipient of the new, and that thus the condition necessary for impression is one in the medium and the inspired prophet. "In such a case I have seen," says the author of "From Matter to Spirit," "every limb thrown into strong convulsive action, as if the unseen influence must permeate every nerve and fibre before the power wielding it could obtain full control of the wires of the human electric telegraph."—(p. 270.) The ancient oracles were generally thrown into convulsions before they gave utterances, and convulsions often precede the trance,—a state particularly favourable to the influx of this spirit. This influx "is often disturbed by the entrance of a third person."—(p. 205.) The sun, the source, as we have seen, of all power, physical and mental, in the human body, "is always given in modern spiritual experience as the material outbirth of the Highest Power, the first remove from pure spirit."—(p. 208.)

As regards the nature of the Intelligence it appears to depend entirely upon the character of the brain from which it emanates, and upon the knowledge possessed by the mind with which the medium or other member of the circle may at the time be *en rapport*. There is ground also for rendering it highly probable that whatever knowledge man has once possessed, whatever discoveries he has once made, are preserved in the spirit atmosphere, or in some organizations with which this atmosphere is in union. Of course then the revelations we receive are various in proportion to the organizations through which they come to us, and the source from which they are received; and no wonder therefore that they are very conflicting. First as to the instruments through which we may receive them. The author of "Adam Bede" observes, "we do not hear that Memnon's statue gave forth its melody at all under the rushing of the mightiest wind, or in response to any other influence divine or human than certain short-lived sunbeams of morning; and we must learn to accommodate ourselves to the discovery that some of those cunningly-fashioned instruments called human souls have only a very limited range of music, and will not vibrate in the least under a touch that fills others with tremulous rapture or quivering agony."* So also, although some, as we have seen, have superior power, the great majority of organizations under the influx of the spirit atmosphere have quite as limited a range, and they can reflect only so much of other minds as the peculiar structure of their own permits. Thus we are told by Mrs. de Morgan "that no *surname* could be given through Jane's mediumship," ("From Matter to Spirit," p. 21,) and that a similar limitation of faculty applies to every phase of mediumship. "We have reason, then, to believe," she says, "that the spirit or communicating power is cognizant of *all* the different forms in which truths may be conveyed through a variety of mediums, but that each medium is chosen for a special quality, which enables him to transmit the sentiment required."—(72.) "I would say then that the elementary idea or truth sought to be conveyed does not originate with the medium; the language, spelling, and form of expression are his or hers."—(81.) As to the mode of inspiration or influx, we are told that "Spirits take the place of an earthly mesmeriser."—(116.)

As touching the source from which "Intelligence" is derived, Mrs. de Morgan tells us, "Many considerations yet remained, and many experiments were still to be tried, before we could have full reason for believing that another intelligence was concerned, or, in other words, that an invisible being directed the operations of the telegraph wire, whose mechanism was in our own organisation."—(p. 88.) * * * "The instances already given, and which might be supported by hundreds besides, prove that their source is not to be found in the medium or in any other member of the circle. The

* Adam Bede, vol. i., p. 177.

communications are coherent and intelligible; often too, quite new to every person present. It seems then not a hasty assumption that they are the work of an intelligent unseen being, acting by means of a force similar to mesmerism upon the system of the medium."—(p. 96.) "The mesmeric force or fluid, or one whose effects on the system are precisely similar, but perhaps more refined, is that by which all the operations of mediumship are carried on, *and the source from which it immediately flows is an unseen and intelligent being, asserting itself to be a spirit, which has quitted the material earthly form.*"—(p. 100.)

May not then this force be an emanation from all brains, the medium increasing its density so as to allow others present to come into communion with it, and the intelligence, "new to every person present," that of some brain in the distance acting through this source upon the mind of the medium or others of the circle? A. J. Davis, the Seer, says, "My information is not derived from any persons that exist in the sphere into which my mind enters; but is the law of truth, emanating from the Great Positive Mind. * * * I pass from the body with a desire for a particular kind of information. This desire attracts the particular kind of truth of which I would be informed, separates it from all other things, and causes it to flow into the mind." *

The "Spirits" no more seem to agree among themselves in the disembodied state than they did while in the body, in fact they reflect every shade of opinion, and every creed in religion, and "Mary Jane" was quite as communicative when appealed to as Mary Jane, as when addressed as dear Spirit; she also played a good hand at whist, and dominoes with the faces turned down, and we are told that the more

* "Principles of Nature."

the room was inhabited during the day the stronger the power. It is found that the Mahomedan can "communicate" with Mahomed, and a Catholic with every Saint in the calendar; and the Archangel Raphael and St. Michael are quite as willing to hold converse as St. Paul; and friends living with friends and relatives departed, and even with those it has turned out were not departed; and we are told by Allen Kardic, (p. 870,) that even "if a person invoke a myth or allegorical person, he will get an answer in the name of that person." In fact, the "spirits" are more given to "personation" than our most corrupt electoral constituencies. What really seems to take place is, that the "communications" represent or reflect the mind of the medium, or of others present, or of absent persons with whom they most sympathise in feeling and idea, and with whom, from certain other natural causes, they are most *en rapport*. As A. J. Davis tells us, they desire a *particular kind* of information, and the desire attracts the particular kind, and causes it to flow into the mind, from some other mind in which such ideas are prominent. Thus we get "Scripture" *reflected* in every varying sect and denomination, and all its facts and allusions, and then reasoning in the usual vicious circle we find Scripture brought as a proof of the truth of those "reflections," and the "reflections" as evidences of the truth of revealed religion. In this way also Spiritualism is made use of as a means for retaining and supporting all the childish superstitions of the infancy of the race. We know that the world, and all of which we are conscious, is the manifestation of One Divine Power everywhere present—"of one great central force, whose origin is in the will of the Most High." We know that our likes and antipathies, our personal and social relations, and our ideas of good and evil, are purely subjective, and have no existence out of ourselves;

and yet all those feelings and prejudices, which are merely human relations, and have no existence *per se*, are carried by the "spirits" into their *upper* spheres, and we hear of "earth-clinging" and "earth-tending" spirits, and that matter is "gross" and spirit "pure"; and that the farther we get away from earth, the nearer we are to heaven, for that heaven is *above*, although, with reference to this earth and the movement on its axis, what is above one twelve hours is below the next. "Souls quite earthly," we are told by Mrs. de Morgan, "wrap themselves in the nerve-spirit, and *give thereby* the characteristic form to their spirit. By the aid of this substance, they can make themselves seen, heard, and felt by men."—("From Matter to Spirit," p. 185.)

Professor de Morgan tells us in his admirable Preface that "the worthy Priest, Jean Meslier, (the author of a book called 'Good Sense,' which had a considerable circulation in its day,) to whom there was no God, knew how the universe would have been fashioned if there had been one: he looked at the First Cause from an earlier point of view."—(Ibid, p. 85.) So the Spiritualists are not satisfied with what they see of God's work here, they think that in many things he was evidently in the wrong, and they have created *a very superior world indeed*, and called it heaven. Here the great sustaining and directing Power, of which the whole Universe, with its countless suns and systems, is but a manifestation, is represented as sitting upon a throne, with ministering angels, in the style of an Eastern monarch, with feelings and ideas not greatly differing. It is into this sphere, I presume, that Professor de Morgan finds it so "ponderously difficult" to enter with his wife and the "Spirits," and it is here certainly that Mrs. de Morgan, so candid and philosophical in her remarks, so correct generally in her observation, appears to lose herself, seeking a resting place for all her better feelings and higher aspirations in company with the *female* mind in general. I agree with her, however, entirely in what follows:—"I have tried to show, that both by reasoning from the phenomena, and by the assertions of the unseen influences, we are led to conclude that the world of spirit is as the vitalizing and forming soul of which the outer world is the material husk. If this be so, it follows as a consequence that every object in creation outlies and typifies its animating cause in the world of spirit. And so every created thing represents some spirit power, each *power* being a modification of the one great central force, whose origin is in the will of the Most High."—(p. 206.)

But here the "animating cause" is said to be "spirit"—"a modification of the one great central force," not spirits, and in case of the natural birth, life and the "spirit" are always transmitted through organization; but there is no evidence of continued organization in the supposed birth into the spirit world. We find no evidence of any intelligent "object," or individuality "outlying and typifying its emanating cause," except the human body, and such *perhaps* as the human will may have the power of forming out of what I have called the mental, thought, or spirit atmosphere, the result of general cerebration. If also spirits existed, in the number they are supposed to do by spiritualists, in and around our atmosphere, would not the fact become evident to our men of science, by their action on light and other imponderables? It is true that we may ask the same with respect to our "cerebration" atmosphere; but the existence of such atmosphere is being made more and more evident through the "sensitives" of Baron Reichenbach and by mesmerisers generally.

It is true that the believers in the "Spirits" are greatly on the increase both in this country and America. The New

England Spiritualists' Association affirms that half the members of Congress and the State Legislatures, as well as half the scientific and literary men of America, are Spiritualists.[*] Probably far the greater number of these, having witnessed the phenomena, and finding that they cannot all be ascribed to fraud or self-delusion, believe in spirits, because they do not know to what else the power and intelligence manifested can be ascribed.

Investigators into Spiritual Manifestations who have rejected the Notion of Spirits.

But there are many investigators who discard the notion of spirits. Thus the author of "Mary Jane; or, Spiritualism Chemically Explained." He believes the influence to be an Odylic emanation from his wife, and entirely dependent upon her for its existence. He says, "I have seen a table move, totally alone; and a chair move, totally alone; move, just as you see a leaf carried along by the wind on a turnpike-road, and I have reasonable conversations with Mary Jane whenever I please;—but I have neither seen nor heard anything to convince me, in the slightest degree, that Mary Jane is the spirit of a deceased person. It is only a hitherto unexplained phenomenon of nature, which, until chemists and scientific men analyse, will be made use of to get money from the many."—(p. 301.) * * * "What, then, is this mysterious being? I will explain to you my version of it—premising that science has an immense, an enormous, and a most invaluable field for discovery in its researches into the nature of it; and that if ever it is taken up by scientific men in the manner it deserves to be, more light will be thrown on the generation and subsequent changes and progressive perfection

[*] Edinburgh Review, October, 1865.

of organic bodies of all sorts, and in the action of food and medicines, and very probably on the causes of the motions of the planetary bodies, than by any study that has hitherto occupied the scientific world."—(p. 925.) The writer then lays down sixteen propositions that he considers proved by the phenomena he has not only witnessed but apparently investigated. I need give only a few of these:—

4. "When these vapours (which Reichenbach calls Odylic,) emanate from certain persons, who appear to have phosphorus in excess in the system, they form a positively living, thinking, acting body of material vapour, able to move a heavy table, and to carry on a conversation, &c., &c., &c.

8. "That this Odylic being thinks and feels exactly as the persons from whose bodies it emanates: that it possesses all the senses—seeing, hearing, smelling, tasting, feeling, and thinking;—that it makes up for the muscular organs of speech, by either an electrical power of rapping, or by guiding the medium's hand, or by direct writing with pen and pencil.

9. "That its power of sight is electrical, for it can see under a domino, or what is in the adjoining room—in short, where the human eye cannot.

14. "That its conversations with different persons will be responsive to the affections, the sentiments, and the religious belief of each person it is talking with, although they are drawn from one common source—the Odylic vapour concentrated at, or with which the table is charged—and although those religious creeds are entirely at variance. And if asked for the name of the (pre-supposed) spirit, it will give the name either of the desired relative, or of some high authority (on religious matters) in the specific creed of the person making the enquiry.

15. "That, from various concurrent testimony, it appears fully proved that this Odylic vapour possesses the power of

taking the shape of hands, arms, dress, &c., and even of an entire person, dressed, &c.

16. "That, nevertheless, the high thought, philosophy, independence, conciseness, and deep reflection evinced by many of the answers and sentiments expressed by the Odylic fluid, point to its connection with a general thought atmosphere, as all-pervading as electricity, and which possibly is in itself, or is in intimate connection with, the principles of causation of the whole universe." *

But this Author is not the only person who has investigated these "modern spiritual manifestations," and who, seeing and believing the phenomena, yet does not believe in "the spirits." A Mr. William Robert Bertolacci has written a little book, called "Christian Spiritualism," in which he details his experiences. He seems to think that the time is come, or fast coming, when God is about "to pour out His Spirit on all flesh." He says, "It is thus that, at this time, when the resources of material science, in their all but miraculous nature and the astounding rapidity of their succession, seem to be drawing to a close, that the most widespread manifestations of an invisible power that have ever been heard of, are sent to this globe of ours, to show us that there still exists an order of things far surpassing the sphere of our temporal reason, and capable of subverting all the theories which we, in the vanity of our material science, have laid down as the 'laws of nature.'"

"Should we not consider these uncalled-for, spontaneous manifestations as forming, at least, a portion of those "signs of the times" which are immediately to precede the spiritual reign of Christ on earth?"†

* Mary Jane; or, Spiritualism Chemically Considered, p. 854.
† Christian Spiritualism, p. 86.

He rejects the intervention of "Souls of the departed," but ascribes most of the phenomena to our own occult spiritual power. This power he considers is to be developed by training, and he has used it in the education of his own family, in the extension and quickening of their natural powers. "After some trials," he says, "my young people were thrown into the magnetic sleep, and in that state could read in books with their eyes bandaged and well padded up—could see and hear things in far-distant places—were made insensible to pain, and deprived of their memory on being awakened, or retained a perfect recollection of all that had passed during their somnambulic state." * * * It was made known to us by the spirit, (not the spirits,) that this power to obstruct or retain the memory could be vastly extended; that the memory with the faculties of perception could be so strengthened as to make the education of our young people the easiest of all things—an amusement, a real recreation—instead of being, as it is now, a slow, tedious and fatiguing process." * * * The acquirements of the somnambulic condition could, with a little pains and perseverance, in the great majority of subjects, be transferred to their normal waking state." By this species of training, by the use of hypnotism, and the power of faith, the abnormal conditions of mesmerism were brought into common daily use, without, so far as I understand, injuring the health or weakening the natural faculties. We are told that whole pages can be retained in the memory by a process of instantaneous "*Psychotyping,*" and the whole process of this kind of clairvoyant education is given at some length. I give only an illustration. "The students are also by the faculty they acquire for receiving inspiration, so perfectly identified with everything belonging to the places spoken of in their study of geography, that they feel as though they were on the spot. So correct are the impressions made by the ubiquitous power of their souls on all the organs of the body in their temporarily perfected condition, that they appear to themselves to be, not where the lessons are going on, but in the very places therein referred to; seeing, hearing, and feeling all that they are required or desirous to see, hear, or feel."

But Mr. Bertolacci not only aided the development of our "latent spiritual faculties" by training and "initiation", but he alleviated pain and cured diseases by communion of the souls of the living. He tells us that "the most miraculous cures can be, and have been lately performed upon persons whose maladies had set at nought all medical science." This has been brought about by the "laying on of hands" or by a certain number of persons forming a chain round the sufferer. Of these cures he gives many instances both within his own family and upon persons without, whose faith in his "spirit of communion" was sufficiently strong. "It is manifest," he says, "that the souls of two or more persons can, during their life on earth, unite and form *one soul* — union is strength; and when that strength is constituted upon the conditions laid down by the Christian Doctrine, it becomes divine power, omnipotent in its principles, and without any limitation in its effects other than that imposed upon it at the time by the degree of the faith of its constituents."

"In consequence of the present degeneration and helpless state of that Church of Redemption, — primitively established by Jesus' direct disciples, but divided at the present day into all sorts of sects, and totally absorbed in vain forms, — every new demonstration of invisible forces is termed, improperly, *supernatural*, by a very great majority of those who witness them, and who, having sought for the cause of them in the erroneous philosophies of bygone ages, have adopted the fallacious creed, that these things are produced by the intervention of the Souls of the departed, *to the exclusion of all participation in them by our own occult spiritual power.*"— (p. 82.) "*The Communion of Saints*," he says, "although on the lips of Christians, has never lately been understood and appreciated, and therefore not in their hearts. They have been taught to understand that Saints are exclusively such persons as, having led a very pious and pure life on earth, are after their death, received *up* into a *local* heaven in the presence of God *infinite*, who, however, is there seated *on a throne surrounded on all sides* by angels, &c.—(p. 82.) Whereas the Apostles taught that they and their strict adherents and followers were Saints. "Our Saviour," he says, "told the Samaritan woman at the well of Sichar, that ' *God is Spirit*,' (not *a* Spirit, which he shows from the Greek to be a misinterpretation), *and that what should be worshipped as God was the Spirit of Truth*. Among the teachings we have received in the inspired writings given to us by the spirit of our communions, has been the following: 'God is not an *extraneous*, individual, isolated Being, but the internal collective, and contiguous life and constitution of all things; not *a* heterogeneous force, but *the* intrinsic strength; not concrete, but abstract; not relative but absolute, as to the principle. I trust that what I have said will go some way towards dispelling, in my readers' minds, those narrow ideas of a materialistic education which leads them to look upon the Deity as of a 'nature distinct' from that of creation; a species of outward looker-on, instead of being, as He is, the intimate constitution, action, life, and intelligence of all things." Mr. Bertolacci admits that it is only by the most determined Will, of which strong faith is the main ingredient, that we can hope to attain to and to persevere in, the "*new life in the Spirit.*" "I have, he says, had to arm myself with the most undaunted determination,"—a Will and determination, I fear, to which very few at present will be found equal; but as I have said before, the power of Will, and of joint Wills, has yet to be tested.

History Confirms the Existence of the Phenomena.

But speaking of the phenomena to which we have adverted, Professor de Morgan tells us very truly, "that historical enquiry shows their existence never to have been entirely unknown."

Thus we have it on the best authority that the Brahmins exhibited before Apollonius of Tyara, who was born four years before Christ, most of the phenomena of modern spiritualism, such as the moving of furniture, levitation, &c., and Apollonius himself is reported to have performed many miracles, and to have wrought many cures. In the East, in his time, these things were Divination and Magic; in the west, especially during the middle ages, Witchcraft. The practice of Magic by the Magi or wise men of the East, was originally the development of the occult powers to which we have referred; it was a reference to a certain vital or spiritual sympathy in the universe, and the attracting of, or union with, these influences or invisible powers, by devotion, and religious rites. Taylor, in his Notes to Pausanias, observes:—"He whose intellectual eye is strong enough to perceive that all things sympathise with all, will be convinced that magic, cultivated by the ancient philosophers, is founded on a theory no less sublime than rational and true. Such a one will consider, as Plotinus observes, the nature of soul everywhere easy to be attracted, when a proper subject is at hand which is easily passive to its influence."

Mesmerism, clairvoyance, divination, and magic were also known to the Egyptians, and formed a considerable part of the mysteries of their Religion.

Of the truth of the prophecies and responses of the Oracles of Greece and the Roman Sybils, the testimony of the Historians is unanimous; the only question was how to account for them. Thus Rollin says, "admitting it to be true some oracles have been followed precisely by the events foretold, we may believe that God, to prevent the blind and sacrilegeous credulity of pagans, has sometimes admitted demons to have knowledge of things to come, and to foretel them distinctly enough. Which conduct of God, though very much above human comprehension, is frequently attested in the Holy Scripture." Dr. Rogers accounts for the oracles as the result of "local mundane emanations," acting upon the nervous system of the Pythia, and developing to a wonderful degree the *pre-sension*, or divining power of the brain, standing, as he affirms it did, in a general relation to all matter. He holds that the controlling action of mind being suspended, her brain became entirely subject to a specific mundane influence, which being reflected back upon the outer world, was called the oracle of the gods,—as in the modern medium it is called "communications from the invisible spirit world."* And Dr. Rogers has probably made a very good guess.

Plato and Pythagoras believed in a "Luciform ætherial vehicle," and Plato says "man does not participate in the divinely-inspired and true prophecy as a reasoning being, but alone when he is either deprived, during sleep, or through sickness, of the exercise of reason, or when by some inspiration, he cannot command himself."

* The Two Worlds, p. 28.

But it was at Alexandria, among the Neo-Platonists as they were called, that we had the fullest development of these phenomena. "We have here," says the Rev. Charles Kingsley, in his Exposition of the Alexandrian Philosophy, "the very phenomena which are puzzling us so now-a-days. They are all there, those modern puzzles, in those old books of the long bygone seekers for wisdom." The Neo-Platonists taught that the soul may in ecstacy attain to divine visions, see beyond the present, and predict the future. Plotinus, generally regarded as the founder of that school, says:— "You ask, how can we know the Infinite? I answer, not by reason. It is the office of reason to distinguish and define. The Infinite, therefore, cannot be ranked among its objects. You can only apprehend the Infinite by a faculty superior to reason, by entering into a state in which you are your finite self no longer, in which the Divine Essence is communicated to you. This is ecstacy. . . . . But this sublime condition is not of permanent duration. It is only now and then that we can enjoy this elevation (mercifully made possible for us) above the limits of the body and the world. I myself have realised it but three times as yet, and Porphyry hitherto not once. All that tends to purify and elevate the mind will assist you in this attainment, and facilitate the approach and recurrence of these happy intervals. There are then, different roads by which this end may be reached. The love of beauty which exalts the poet; that devotion to the One and that ascent of science which makes the ambition of the philosopher; and that love and those prayers by which some devout and ardent soul tends in its moral purity towards perfection. These are the great highways conducting to that height above the actual and the particular, where we stand in the immediate presence of the infinite, who shines out as from the deeps of the soul."

Iamblichus, or the writer of the treatise that bears his name, says:—" The pomp of emperors becomes as nothing in comparison with the glory that surrounds the hierophant. His nature is the instrument of Deity who fills and impels him. Men of this order do not employ in the elevation they experience, the waking senses as do others. They have no purpose of their own, no mastery over themselves. They speak wisdom they do not understand, and their faculties absorbed in a divine power become the utterance of a superior will. * * * Frequently, not merely the ordinary exercise of reason, but sensation and animal life would appear to have been suspended; and the subject of the afflatus has not felt the application of fire, has been pierced with spits, cut with knives, and not been sensible of pain. Yes, often, the more the body and the mind have been alike impeded by vigils and fasts, the more mentally imbecile and ignorant a youth may be who is brought under this influence, the more freely and unmixedly will the divine power be made manifest. So clearly are these wonders the work, not of human skill and wisdom, but of supernatural agency! Characteristics, such as these I have mentioned are the marks of the true inspiration."

Victor Hugo also bears his testimony on this subject— he says, " There is a time when the unknown reveals itself in a mysterious way to the spirit of man. A sudden rent in the veil of darkness will make manifest things hitherto unseen, and then close again upon the mysteries within. Such visions have occasionally the power to effect a transfiguration in those whom they visit. They convert a poor camel-driver into a Mahomet; a peasant girl tending her goats into a Joan of Arc. Solitude generates a certain amount of sublime exultation. It is like the smoke arising from the burning bush.

"A mysterious lucidity of mind results, which converts the student into a seer, and the poet into a prophet: herein we find a key to the mysteries of Horeb, and Ebron, and Ombos; to the intoxication of Castalian laurels, the revelations of the month Busion. Hence too, we have Peleia at Dodona, Phemonoe at Delphos, Trophonius in Zobades, Ezekiel on the Chebar, and Jerome in the Thebais.

"More frequently this visionary state overwhelms and stupifies its victim. There is such a thing as a divine besotedness. The Hindoo fakir bears about with him the burden of his vision, as the Cretin his goitre. Luther holding converse with devils in his garret at Wittenburgh; Pascal shutting out the view of the infernal regions with the screen of his cabinet; the African Obi conversing with the white-faced god Bossum; are each and all the same phenomena, diversely interpreted by the minds in which they manifest themselves, according to their capacity and power. Luther and Pascal were grand, and are grand still; the Obi is simply a poor half-witted creature, &c.

* * * * *

"Reverie, which is thought in its nebulous state, borders closely upon the land of sleep, by which it is bounded as by a natural frontier. The discovery of a new world, in the form of an atmosphere filled with transparent creatures, would be a beginning of a knowledge of the vast unknown. But beyond opens out the illimitable domain of the possible, teeming with yet other beings, and characterised by other phenomena. All this would be nothing supernatural, but merely the occult continuation of the infinite variety of creation."*

* Toilers of the Sea, v. 1., c. 7.

The Manifestations in the Catholic Church.

It is in the history of the Catholic Church among its saints and martyrs that we find the most numerous illustrations and the fullest confirmation of the phenomena of modern spiritualism, but these were misunderstood and misinterpreted by the Church, as they are in the present day by spiritualists. By Protestants they have all been regarded as pious frauds. The study of the subject, however, as a branch of physiology will teach us to be more discriminating. The fact of persons being raised from the ground and borne through the air has been variously attested. "The fact is authentically attested of St. Ignatius of Loyola, St. Dominick, St. Dunstan, St. Francis of Assissium, St. Teresa, St. Cozetan, St. Bernard Ptolemæi, St. Catharine of Ricci, and several others." Calmet remarks, among other instances which came under his own observation:—"I knew a nun, to whom it has often happened, in spite of herself, to see herself thus raised up in the air to a certain distance from the earth; it was neither from choice, nor from any wish to distinguish herself, since she was truly confused at it."*

With respect to what were thought to be miraculous cures, the testimony of the Church is overwhelming. Mr. Lecky, with Middleton, rejects the old Protestant theory, that "miracles became gradually fewer and fewer, till they at last entirely disappeared;" and accepts without reserve the statement of this intrepid writer in his "Free Inquiry," that as far as the Church historians can illustrate or throw light on anything, "there is not a single point in all history so constantly, explicitly, and unanimously affirmed by them all

* The Two Worlds, p. 58.

as the continual succession of these (miraculous) powers through all ages, from the earliest Father who first mentions them down to the time of the Reformation." So far from being "rare and exceptional phenomena," miracles were supposed to be of familiar and daily occurrence in the lives of the early and mediæval saints.* The *British Quarterly Review* for October, 1861, in an article on "Christianity and the true Civilizations," remarks:—"The frequent intervention of supernatural agencies in human affairs was an admitted fact in the faith of the Ancients, and hardly less so in the faith of the Middle Ages. To reject all credence of that nature is peculiar to modern times." Mr. Morison, in his "Life of Saint Bernard," observes:—"Miracles, ghostly apparitions, divine and demoniac interference with sublunary affairs, were matters which a man of the twelfth century would less readily doubt of than of his own existence. To disbelieve such phenomena would have been considered good *primâ facie* evidence of unsoundness of mind."

"Saint Bernard, the most marked representative and fitting type of that central period of the middle ages, had visions and revelations, in which future events were revealed to him, and which he predicted with the greatest particularity and accuracy." His healing power was most extraordinary. Harman, Bishop of Constance, and nine others, kept a diary of what they saw with their own eyes, during his progress through the Rhine country. "Many miracles," they say, "from this time shone forth, which, if we should pass over, the very stones would proclaim. . . . . . The halt, the blind, the deaf, and dumb, were brought from all parts to be touched by Bernard." † We learn that Bernard himself became perplexed

---

* The Contemporary Review, p. 375.
† The Two Worlds, p. 53.

and uneasy at these wonders. He knew that they were not done by his own power, and disclaimed all merit in them. He said:—"I can't think what these miracles mean, or why God has thought fit to work them through such a one as I. I do not remember to have read, not even in Scripture, of anything more wonderful. Signs and wonders have been wrought by holy men and by deceivers. I feel conscious neither of holiness nor deceit. I know I have not those saintly merits which are illustrated by miracles. I trust, however, that I do not belong to the number of those who do wonderful things in the name of God, and yet are unknown to the Lord." *

But we are not dependent upon what are considered to be the fabulous ages of the Roman Catholic Church for an illustration of the curative power that belongs to some individuals. Mr. Valentine Greatrakes, a Protestant gentleman of the county of Waterford, born in 1628, a thoroughly sound Christian and good man, but no Saint, occupying a highly respectable place in society, showed a power quite equal to that related of St. Bernard. An account is given of this gentleman in *Chambers' Journal*, No. 814, and quoted in the Appendix to the Atkinson and Martineau's Letters; Mr. Atkinson having himself considerable mesmeric power in the same way. Mr. Greatrakes, after practising with great success at home, went to England for the purpose of curing the Viscountess Conway of an inveterate headache, in which he failed. But while residing at Ragley, with the Conway family, he cured many hundreds afflicted with various diseases. Lord Conway, in a letter to his brother, thus speaks of the healer:—"I must confess that, before his arrival, I did not believe the tenth part of those things which I have been an eye-witness of. * * * After all, I am far from thinking that his cures are all

* Ibid, p. 55.

miraculous. I believe it is by a *sanative virtue* and a *natural efficiency*, which extends not to all diseases, but is much more proper and effectual to some than to others, as he doth also despatch some with a great deal of ease, and others not without a great deal of pains."

He was invited by the King to London, whither he went, curing very many by the way. There the Royal Society, evidently then young and green, threw the light of their countenance and wisdom upon the matter, publishing some of the cures in their Transactions, and accounting for them as produced by "a sanative contagion in Mr. Greatrake's body, which had an antipathy to some particular diseases and not to others." The "sanative contagion" had an "antipathy" to diseases mostly connected with the nervous system, upon which Mind and Will are known to exercise most influence, the nervous fluid from one body being infused into another. We are told by a contemporary writer, Henry More, mentioned by Southey in his "Omneana," that Greatrakes was successful in "cancers, scrofula, deafness, king's evil, headache, epilepsy, fevers, (though quartan ones,) leprosy, palsy, tympany, lameness, numbness of limbs, stone, convulsions, ptysick, sciatica, ulcers, pains of the body, nay, blind and dumb in some measure, and I know not but he cured the gout."

Mr. Atkinson tells us that "Any change in the nervous condition affects others. I have told you," he says, "how distinctly I felt the commencement of the mesmeric condition in my patient, as of a slight electric shock; and I have been sensible of each change during the sleep, *and of the flowing away of disease*. When diseases are dying out, they influence others. It is even so with a common cold, which passes away to another. And so, likewise, the state of a dying person influences:—flies off, as it were; disturbs or influences the universal medium, and thus reaches those in whom there was *rapport*, if they be in a fit condition to receive."* † It seems from Greatrake's case, that if we can take disease—a feat which is not denied—so also can we take health. ‡

* Man's Nature and Development, p. 279.

† The only ghosts that were considered to be "established" by the "Oxford Ghost Club"—a body formed expressly for the investigation of such superstitious phenomena, were those that appeared at death. The Brain contains a whole reservoir of correlated force called soul or spirit, and as the vital functions cease it must pass away through some other medium. "I have known," says Mr. Atkinson, "a dying child mesmerise a powerful man," (Letters, p. 278,) and from the numerous well-authenticated cases of people appearing to others at their deaths, it would seem that such force was able for a time at least, to retain some kind of identity and individuality and to impress it on others. The most modern ghost of this sort on record with which I am acquainted is the one seen by Dr. Pusey:—"I was," says the reverend doctor, "passing down a somewhat crowded street in Oxford, when I was surprised to perceive at my elbow a man whom I believed to be too ill at the time to leave his bed; he said 'Dr. Pusey, I have been burning in Hell the last hour for that lie I told you (it is supposed in the confessional).' I turned round," the doctor went on to say, "to ask an explanation, but the people pressed upon me, and I lost sight of the figure of the man who accosted me. In great surprise, I hastened to his residence and learnt at his door, that he had been dead about an hour." This anecdote was told to the Sisters in Osnaburg Street, and is taken from the as yet uncontradicted statement made by Miss Goodman, in her "Sisterhoods in the Church of England," p. 25. It is impossible that a man of the well-known character of Dr. Pusey, can have wholly invented this story. The "passing away" of the mental force of his acquaintance may have impressed itself on his mind, with even his last thought; or the ghost only may have been a reality, and the "Hell and Purgatory" the produce merely of a strong faith and imagination.—See Appendix C.

‡ Since this was written, that is, on May 7th, 1866, I attended a lecture at Saint Mary's Hall, Coventry, by a Mr. George Powell, who styles himself Practical Mesmerist, Phrenologist, and Medical Electrician. The lecturer, after a few preliminary remarks to show that vital power was transmissible, as in the well known case of young people sleeping with old ones, &c., &c., proceeded to mesmerise about twenty

Witchcraft.

Witchcraft is now generally believed to be entirely a delusion. But we must recollect that the belief was current throughout, not only Christendom, but the whole world, for many centuries. So late as 1664, two women were condemned at Suffolk, by Sir Matthew Hale, for witchcraft, on the ground—first, that Scripture had affirmed the reality of

---

of the audience, all but one of whom he put to sleep immediately. He then selected six of the most sensitive to illustrate electro-biology, phreno-mesmerism, and mesmerism, in which he showed great power, and was completely successful, to the great amusement, delight, and wonder of the spectators. He then said that if there were any there suffering from pain he could probably dismiss it at once. Only one young gentleman came forward, who had been suffering from tooth ache, he said, all day; the pain was dismissed with a touch, and had certainly not returned when we left the room, probably an hour after. After the lecture, while I was waiting for Mr. Powell, in about a quarter of an hour, he cured two people of tooth ache, one of rheumatism and greatly relieved another, one lady of a pain and lameness in the foot, and another old lady of a bad head ache to which she was subject, and from which she had been suffering all day. I had no opportunity of ascertaining how far these cures were permanent, but Mr. Powell has since supplied me with a number of testimonials and letters of gratitude from persons who profess to have been cured of the most obstinate diseases, of the class mentioned above as cured by Mr. Groatrakes, and which, it was said, had previously resisted all medical treatment. Mr. Powell is a self-educated man, with a full development of the coronal region of the brain, a very large chest, and highly sanguine temperament. He discovered his power by accident, while staying at a farm-house and pretending to mesmerise a gentleman's knee for rheumatism. His bodily system seems to generate immense vital power, which he can transmit to others; and we must infer, I think, from these experiments that in most nervous cases it is the want of vital power in the part affected that causes the disease.

witchcraft; and secondly, that the wisdom of all nations had provided laws against persons accused of the crime. Sir Thomas Browne, the well-known author of the "Religio Medici," was called as a witness at the trial, and swore "that he was clearly of opinion that the persons were bewitched." Not only so, but More and Cudworth, both of them belonging to the enlightened band of Cambridge Platonists, strongly expressed their belief in the reality of witchcraft; and more than all, Joseph Glanvil, the author of the "Scepsis Scientifica," and the most daring theological thinker, perhaps, of his time, wrote a special defence of the decaying superstition, under the name of "Sadducismus Triumphatus," probably the ablest book ever published in its defence. So far as mere arguments were concerned, the divines seemed to have it all their own way. "The books in defence of the belief were not only far more numerous than the later works against it, but they also represented far more learning, dialectic skill, and even general ability." The mass of evidence seemed in favour of it. "Those who lived when the evidences of witchcraft existed in profusion, and attracted the attention of all classes and of all grades of intellect, must surely have been as competent judges as ourselves of the question, were it merely a question of evidence. . . . . It is, I think, difficult to examine the subject with impartiality without coming to the conclusion, that the historical evidence establishing the existence of witchcraft is so vast and varied, that it is impossible to disbelieve it without what, on other subjects, we should deem the most extraordinary rashness."* It is highly probable, indeed, that the people of those times were not such fools as we take them to be. Witchcraft appears to have been based upon the occult powers to which we have referred, and which were

Lecky on Rationalism, from *The Contemporary Review*, part 8.

then as much misinterpreted as they are now and have always been. "The facts, misunderstood, were ridden by theories, and viewed in the light of a baneful superstition, compounded of Paganism, Judaism, and a corrupted Christianity."* The author of "Mary Jane" (p. 801) thus identifies witchcraft with the modern phenomena; he says:—"The female of all animals, as well as man, is so constituted for the purposes of gestation and lactation as to eliminate more liquids, and probably consequently more vapours—that hence more women are mediums than men. That old women, from their sedentary habits, probably secreted more phosphorus, or at least eliminated it in confined rooms, where it produced those effects which we witness, and so becoming conscious of a power which they understood nothing of the nature of, they used it to get a livelihood, and thus, poor things, from Moses's time downwards, got burnt as witches; and there is no doubt, that when they saw the extraordinary phenomena they could produce, and that the church, and the magistrates, and the judges, and the mob, all declared that they were witches and possessed by evil spirits, that the poor things really believed it—the wrong persons were burned, in my opinion." Still there was Scripture warrant for what was done, for we are told (Lev. xx. 27) that "a man also, or woman, that hath a familiar spirit, shall surely be put to death."

The Abnormal Mental Powers of the Founders of Sects, &c.

Abnormal powers attended many great and good men and founders of sects, some phase of such powers being more strongly developed in some cases than in others, giving the name to particular sects, such as Quakers, Shakers, Jumpers,

* The Two Worlds, p. 102.

Methodists, &c., according as the powers of efflux and influx first displayed themselves, and which were afterwards thought necessary and therefore took that form in the disciples. For the history of such cases, and of many others connected with this subject, I must refer the reader to the admirable compendium from which I have previously quoted, called "The Two Worlds, the Mental and the Spiritual," published by Pitman, Paternoster Row. This book shows great research and is admirably and candidly written, although in support of individual spirit manifestations; but I think the facts will better bear the interpretation that I have put upon them. I would especially call attention to the fact that all the manifestations, whether subjective or objective, reflected the opinions of either the district, country, or age, and were warm from the minds of persons living, and not from such as had passed into another sphere, where they might be supposed to have gained fresh knowledge. The only "spirit" with which the world can really be said to be familiar is one having a goat's head with the extremities of the satyr of the heathen mythology, and whether he, or *she* most probably, is a reflex of our own minds—"a foregone conclusion established and favoured by the then dominant theology," or a real objective existence, must be left for each person to determine for himself. The author of "The Two Worlds" says, "True Spiritualism is God in the Soul;"—in this at least I heartily agree with him. The same writer, speaking of Irving's time, says:—"Nor is the healing by spiritual power the only point of correspondence in the spiritual manifestations of Mr. Irving's time and of our own. In both periods we have spiritual utterances independent of the volition of the speaker, in the native, in foreign, and in unknown tongues; writing under spiritual influence and from spiritual dictation; sudden inward illumination and impression; and discernment of thoughts, and answers to questions, both mental and oral. In the spiritual utterances then and now we find the same general character of virtue and piety, with occasional inconsistencies and discrepancies, and other indications of a 'varying origin'; evidencing that the same differences in character and state which we find among men in the natural world prevail also in the spiritual world." Irving himself, we are told by Mr. Baxter, regarded the manifestations as of " varying origin, that the utterances at one time might be of God, and at another time of Satan, even in the same person."

John Wesley's opinion of the manifestations that attended his church appear to have been very similar. The following is an extract from his Journal:—" I. God suddenly and strongly convinced many that they were lost sinners; the natural consequences whereof were sudden outcries and strong bodily convulsions. II. To strengthen and encourage them that believed, and to make his work more apparent, He favoured several of them with divine dreams, and others with trances or visions. III. In some of these instances, after a time, nature mixed with grace. IV. Satan likewise mimicked the work of God in order to discredit the whole work; and yet it is not wise to give up this part any more than to give up the whole. At first it was doubtless wholly from God. It is partly so at this day; and he will enable us to discern how far, in every case, the work is pure, and where it mixes or degenerates." This very correctly characterises what takes place at Revivals at the present time. It is a spirit circle on a large scale, and influx or inspiration, or what is " burns in " on the mind is the reflex of the public opinion present, often mixed with other occult powers.

One of the most peculiar outbreaks of this kind is what has been called, the " Preaching Epidemic," of Sweden, in 1842, described by Mary Howitt. Fortunately we have the aid of a very sensible man in the investigation of this psychological phenomenon, who, if it was of divine origin as was generally supposed, was yet bent upon determining the conditions under which it took place. Dr. J. A. Butsch, bishop of Skara, in Westgöthland, reports to the archbishop of Upsala, on the subject. "The bishop was of opinion that it was a disease originally physical, but affecting the mind in a peculiar manner. He arrived at this conclusion by attentively studying the phenomenon itself. At all events, bodily sickness was an ingredient in it, as was proved from the fact that, although every one affected by it, in describing the commencement of their state, mentioned a spiritual excitement as its original cause, close examination proved that an internal bodily disorder, attended by pain, had preceded or accompanied this excitement. Besides, there were persons who, against their own wills, were affected by the quaking fits which were one of its most striking early outward symptoms, without any previous religious excitement; and these, when subjected to medical treatment, soon recovered. The bishop said that the effects corresponded very much with what he had heard and read respecting animal magnetism." The probability is that the internal bodily disorder was the "medium," or induced condition, by which the peculiar spiritual atmosphere entered their nervous systems.

The Constitution of the Medium.

We are told in the "Two Worlds" "that there are persons in some way peculiarly constituted, whose presence appears to furnish conditions requisite to enable Spirits to act upon Matter, or to manifest their agency in any way cognizable to man. In what this peculiarity consists, whether it be chemical, electrical, magnetic, odylic, or some combination of

A MEDIUM NECESSARY IN EVERY CIRCLE.   188

these, or somewhat else, it would lead me too far from my
present purpose to consider. At present, I would only point
out the fact that the presence of one such person at least is
necessary in every circle before any spiritual manifestation can
be obtained. Such persons in past times have been variously
called 'seers,' 'prophets,' 'revelators,' 'inspired persons,'
'gifted persons,' 'instruments,' &c. They are now called
Mediums." If our author would say " to enable *spirit*," the
result of cerebration, to act upon matter, and not "spirits," I
should agree with him. My theory is that the medium, from
peculiarity of constitution, intensifies the spirit atmosphere,
so as to bring the other members of the circle into communion
with it, * and that the manifestations are the often unconscious

---

* As a mere physical illustration of how spiritual force may be en
rapport with some minds and not with others, let me mention an interesting experiment by Professor Tyndall. He says:—"Let me give
you one other illustration of the influence of Synchronism on musical
vibrations. Here are three small gas-flames inserted in three glass
tubes of different lengths. Each of those flames can be caused to emit
a musical note, the pitch of which is determined by the length of the
tube surrounding the flame. The shorter the tube the higher the pitch.
The flames are now silent within their respective tubes, but each of
them can be caused to respond to a proper note sounded anywhere in
this room. I have here an instrument called a syren, by which I can
produce a powerful musical note. Beginning with a low pitch, and
ascending gradually to a higher one, I finally reach the note of the
flame in the longest tube. The moment it is reached, the flame bursts
into song. I stop and re-excite the syren, to enable you to hear that its
note and the flame's note are identical. But the other flames are still
silent within their tubes. I urge the instrument on six higher notes;
the second flame has now started, and the third alone remains. But a
still higher note starts it also. Thus, as the sound of the syren rises
gradually in pitch, it awakens every flame in passing, by striking it with
a series of waves whose periods of recurrence are similar to its own."
Lecture delivered in the Royal Institution, January 19th, 1866, on
"The Relations of Radiant Heat to Chemical Constitution, Colour,
and Texture."—*Fortnightly*, February 15.

reflex of their mental states, intensified by the influx from without. This influx or inspiration is poured out only through the organization or vessels present, and is mixed with what is found 'there. From predominating propensities and active passions we get devilish manifestations, and *vice versa* when the æsthetic, the religious, or the moral feelings predominate. But we not only have the reflex of the minds forming this circle, but often that of others not present with whom these are *en rapport* by means of the all pervading spirit atmosphere. Of course the difficulty here, and that which has necessitated the assumption of separate individual spirits, is the existence of *consciousness* and *will* without any of the persons present being conscious of exercising either. The difficulty, however, is not greater than in the unconsciousness that attends somnambules and the mesmeric states, and in the unconscious cerebration which regulates the great majority of all our actions supposed to be voluntary, and which originally were so. From having been drilled hard in Murray in my school days, I can now repeat the whole of my adverbs, prepositions, and conjunctions, while thinking of something else, in the same way that ladies will play polkas and quadrilles, or other familiar tunes, and carry on a conversation at the same time. The difficulty is merely with the Will, because we do not at present understand what is its power, or the nature and extent of its action. Physiologists tell us that although the action of the cerebral hemispheres and many other parts of the nervous system must be attended by sensibility and consciousness, still there must be a great generation of nervous force attended with no consciousness, and that the channels through which this discharges itself depends upon the nature and acquired tendencies of the organism. Can we say what is the Will power of Somnambules? It is Will power that has created and sustains the

Universe, and who shall say what may be the limit and amount that may be exercised by each individuality, or how this individual force may act when joined to others. But if there is a difficulty attending my explanation, that attending the theory of spirits that have passed away—the existence of disembodied sentient being,—is "ponderous" indeed.

The Spirits; their Abodes and Occupations.

We are told by Mrs. de Morgan that "Within the body is the soul, which passes away at the first change, death, and, animated by the spirit, becomes the body of the new life. * * The internal of the man, is the external of the spirit, and extending the principle from individuals to the mass, we find that the inner state of the material world forms the outer or phenomenal form of the spiritual sphere." * * * ("From Matter to Spirit," p. 208.) "Clairvoyants also assert," we are told, "that their perceptions resemble those of persons immediately after death, when the soul has become the body, and the entranced person holds converse with those dwellers in the spirit spheres with whom he is in harmony or affinity." * * * (Ibid, p. 209.) "Whatever the impressing spirit thinks, the medium sees, and the same idea may be conveyed by saying, that, as every thought or feeling in the earth-life leaves its impress on the soul, the soul, when it becomes the body of the spirit, has only to recall the memory of any particular condition to produce the appearance required." (p. 204.) Bacon thought that the spirit evolved from the body is the body of the mind; that as the body is to this spirit, so is this spirit to mind. * There seems considerable similarity between the two ideas, but Mrs. de

---

* Man's Nature and Development, p. 270.

Morgan goes considerably farther, and describes the whole process of the new birth into the spirit world, which persons whose spiritual eyes are opened have repeatedly witnessed. It has a marked resemblance to our birth into this world, some of the spirits of the departed generally attending as midwives; and we are told that sensitives can always distinguish these new-born spirits, and also that "a person whose spiritual eye is opened will always see the spirits with whom he is *en rapport*." (Ibid, p. 247.) However, the whole process of the "new birth" so much resembles the old that the "spirits" cannot be said to be more than the children of those from whom they had their birth on earth, and can no more be said to be the same people than the son can be said to be his own father. The Spirits so born are not called away, as we might expect, to inhabit other worlds in this illimitable universe, but remain in different *spheres*, in close contiguity with this earth, the distance varying according as the spirit retains more or less of its gross, "earth-clinging tendencies:" the best among them, however, are not so far off but that for half-a-crown, paid to a medium, they may generally be summoned to "communicate," or to answer any questions that may be put to them, and from their replies we may justly conclude that they strictly limit themselves to the capacity of their questioners. The occupations of those "earth-tending spirits" who continue in close contiguity with this earth, do not seem always of the most dignified or desirable character. They are in attendance on former friends and relations,—at the elbow of the new husband or wife who is saying just the same things over again as were said on the former happy occasion; or they are putting good or evil thoughts into people's minds, or attending the tables of spiritualist circles, or waiting upon the sick or dying. And, as the soul-bodies of all who have existed are present, they must be rather thick upon the ground, so that we may soon be again occupied with the questions that so much interested the middle ages, as to how many angels can stand upon the point of a needle at once, or, if a spirit were in *vacuo*, whether the void could truly be called perfect? Mr. Gully says, "spiritual bodies that have quitted fleshly bodies may be at work. I, for one, wish that it may be proved to be so; for a more solemn discovery than that of a means of communication between embodied and disembodied sentient beings cannot be imagined." The discovery, if it has been made, has certainly not yet been attended with all the solemnity that Mr. Gully anticipated; and as to the communication between the embodied and the disembodied, one can at least imagine many occasions in which it would not be thought desirable. It is probable that nothing in the world of mind worth retaining has ever been lost to the race: it has been preserved to us in improved organizations, by tradition, and by printing; and the intercourse we can all have with the minds of the great and good that have departed, in our libraries, furnishes a higher response than anything that has yet been got out of the tables.

The pictures which the less gross spirits give of "the future life" in their *higher* spheres, show such a world as poetical *young* ladies would have made this had they been consulted about it, full of flowers and green fields and glory; but when such pictures and other information cannot be received *literally* by such sensible, grown-up women as Mrs. de Morgan, they are accepted symbolically, that is, they are translated into a language of preconceived ideas.

But spiritualism, we are told, *proves* the existence of "a future state": it certainly may make people doubt, for the first time perhaps, whether *such* a future state is desirable. It is also said to prove the Immortality of the Soul; now, nothing is better proved than that all force or spirit is persistent or indestructible; it is the form only that changes; and spiritualism furnishes no evidence that the form the spirit takes in the spirit world is more immutable than the one it had in this world. As to the spirit being born again into another world, the nature of spirit is that it is always being born again, and it is known to us only through such new births or changes. It is the question of identity only that remains, and each person must settle that for himself; only I would suggest that a spirit's knowledge of what took place in this world is no *proof* that it was in any way connected with the events, much less of its being identical with the person to whom they happened. The Immortality of the Soul, or to what extent our Identity may be retained in the future, as regards *proof*, is left by spiritualism exactly where it was. The tendency of opinion amongst men of science of the present day, however, is rather against the retention of Identity. They seem rather to agree with Dr. Louis Büchner, who says, "L'immortalité de la force indique, de la même manière que la permanence de la matière, un enchaînement sans commencement ni fin de cause primitive et d'effet: l'eternité, la perpetuité et l'immortalité, non pas assurément de l'être pris isolément ou de l'individu, mais de la masse ou de tout l'ensemble. Plus la science naturelle avance dans ces recherches, plus elle apprend à connaître que rien ne se crée et rien ne disparait, mais que tout reste dans un cercle eternel qui se subvient à lui-même, dans lequel tout commencement est une fin et toute fin un nouveau commencement."*

The occult powers have been present in the world from the earliest ages, but the world has never yet been able to receive them. In the East—in India, they dictated the

* Science et Nature.

Vedas, they being the revelations of Seers who attained to inspiration in the Trance, in which state they were supposed to attain to inward sight and to communicate directly with God; the highest good, it was thought, to which man can attain on earth. They left a system of castes, based upon their religion, which stereotyped the then existing civilization. In Egypt the same powers were used to extend and confirm the authority of the priesthood, which authority, through Moses, who graduated in their colleges, has been handed down to the present day. In early Christendom among its Saints this power did God's work, among the Witches afterwards it did the Devil's; and now when it has again broken out under the form of modern "spiritual manifestations," the question is whose work is it doing? As to checking, as it is supposed to do, the materialistic tendencies of the age,—for one convert it makes ten scoffers, and as the power is not understood, it is fast assisting the over brain-work of the age to fill our mad-houses. Mediumship is but too often a form of disease, arising from a too unequal distribution of the force received into the body, the nervous system unduly predominating. The best subjects for spiritual manifestations are already bordering on madness, from exaltation of temperament or nervous susceptibility, and the "influx" or indeed the additional excitement about ghosts and devils and the spirits of departed friends is all that is required to push them over. Our greatest poet says:—

> "Great wits are to madness near allied:
> The lunatic, the lover, and the poet,
> Are of imagination all compact!"

And Plato says, "The greatest blessings we have spring from madness, when granted by Divine bounty:" probably alluding to some of the higher forms of spiritual manifestation in his day. Accordingly we find that the lunatic asylums in America are overcharged with the victims of Spiritualism. In the *Times* of April 8rd, 1869, is the following:—" The *Courier* of Lyons states, that in one of the private lunatic asylums, in the neighbourhood of that city, there are not less than forty persons confined, labouring under mental aberration caused by spiritualism." And a month before, in the same paper, we had the following:—

"'*Demonomophy*' in France. The lunatic asylums of France have of late received large additions to their inmates from the admission of various patients whose maladies have been the result of the new-fangled doctrines of spiritualism, including the usual accompaniments of table-turning, mediums, rappings, and intercourse with demons." * A lady who signs herself "Comfort," in a letter to Mrs. Newton Crosland, given by Mrs. de Morgan, describes the process by which this kind of monomania—one form of this particular kind of insanity, takes place; she says, "I have many and many times started up and walked rapidly into the fresh air, using every power of my mind to withdraw myself from the inner into the external life; but in vain; a power far mightier than my own will had commenced its lovely, mysterious work within me, and was moulding my mind and body into that mystic organism for which we at the present day have no other term, or, perhaps, dare use no other, than medium of spirit. So many of these organisms are being developed at the present time that it is the bounden duty, especially of medical men, to calmly and philosophically investigate the phenomena." †

I think so indeed! Still if this power were understood and used instead of abused, it might do as much for the cure of

* Mary Jane, p. 317. † From Matter to Spirit, p. 285.

insanity, by supplying healthy brain-power, as it now does to drive people mad. Judge Edmonds, the American great spiritualist authority, writes:—"I know something of the disease of insanity. My professional and judicial life has compelled me to study it, and I have communed with many who died insane; and I am convinced that there are no means known among men that can do so much to cure and eradicate the disease as spiritual intercourse well understood and wisely guided." If "well understood and wisely guided," instead of "spiritual intercourse" we should use the "influx" of healthy cerebration, then I should quite agree with the Judge in its curative influence, especially in this disease.

The Rationale of the Spiritual Phenomena.

The spiritual hypothesis places us in very little better position with respect to mental science than we were with respect to physical science when every unknown cause was supposed to be some God or Spirit; we had gods of the winds, of the thunder, and of the sea, and smaller spirits for the streams, &c., and subject, not to any known law, but only to their caprice. But if we can lay these spirits, and discover the laws upon which these abnormal powers, and extraordinary phenomena are dependent, we may add the most useful chapter of all to the book of science. We have discovered the law of gravitation, and we now want a Newton in the department of mind. We want now to know the law, not of gravitation, but of Levitation, by which Brahmins, and Saints, and Mr. Home, and tables float. We want to know the exact conditions under which vital force becomes mental or conscious force, and of its re-correlation into unconsciousness in sleep or under pressure on the brain; or when it passes from the brain into the body through the nerves or directly into space. Swedenborg tells us that "thought is presence;" but we want to know more definitely how mind is brought into the presence of mind, how brain acts upon brain, through an independent thought or spirit medium, and what is the result in increased power or otherwise by joining brain with brain; and what is the nature and extent of will power—automatic or unconscious, and conscious; under what conditions one passes into the other, and through what mediums will—conscious or unconscious, can act, and at what distances? What also is the healing power possessed by such men as Greatrakes and in a minor degree by modern mesmerists? These and many other things suggested by mesmerism, clairvoyance, and the "modern spiritual manifestations," apparently within the boundaries of our faculties, are now pressing for explanation and reduction to law, and when that is accomplished, or even investigated, the power of mind will be as greatly and rapidly increased as physical power has been by recent discoveries in steam and electricity. The author of "Spiritualism Chemically Considered" tells us that the "manifestations" increased with use, and decreased, till they entirely disappeared, when no longer attended to; and Mr. Bertolacci need the abnormal powers in his family by training and initiation. The investigation of these psychological phenomena on a physiological basis would show us the conditions on which the formation of a strong and healthy mind depends. The general health is dependent on ozone; where iodine is deficient we have cretinism, and where phosphorus is in excess, madness. Mr. Kyan tells us that "If the brain of a man has only one-and-a-half per cent. of phosphorus, he is an imbecile; if he has two to two-and-a-half per cent., he is of sound intellect; if three per cent., a degree of eccentricity; if four to four-and-a-half per cent., a madman." As certain elements in the soil are necessary to the growth of wheat, so certain ingredients in the food, and even in the atmosphere, are necessary to thought. We want the physical facts bearing on the production of the human intellect. In the dry atmosphere of America the nervous system unduly predominates, and in England John Bull's mind is getting smothered in fat,* and we get genius at the expense of the vital functions. But we must learn how to combine the temperaments of genius with robust health, and bring back Holy to its original meaning—healthy. The germ of the oak seems little influenced by the surrounding pabulum in the acorn, upon the chemical changes in which its growth depends; but the human germ depends more upon the woman than the man. It is fed upon the mental and vital forces of the mother, and yet there has been no attempt to dictate what those forces shall be. If we would make Shakspeares and Newtons we must begin with the germ and race, but the coming child is left to chance, and when it does come there is no attempt to gauge its capabilities, to train its special faculties, and to save it an infinity of pain and labour through life by starting it in the right direction: or at least what effort is made is altogether unscientific in its character, judged even by the light we already possess on such subjects. Few get right aims, and the failures in life are in proportion. No doubt we are

* "We, in our dry atmosphere, are getting too nervous, haggard, dyspeptic, attenuated, unsubstantial, theoretic, and need to be made grosser. John Bull, on the other hand, has grown bulbous, long-bodied, short-legged, heavy-witted, material, and, in a word, too intensely English. In a few more centuries, he will be the earthliest creature ever the world saw. Heretofore, Providence has obviated such a result by timely intermixtures of alien races with old English stock; so that each successive conquest of England has proved a victory, by the revivification and improvement of its native manhood. Cannot America and England hit upon some scheme to secure even greater advantages to both nations?"—*Our Old Home*, vol. i., p. 99. By Nathaniel Hawthorne.

bordering upon a great advance. With a Psychology based on Physiology we can have any kind of men we like, with any type of body, and any kind of feeling. At present man is little better than an animal of the pig and peacock species; building a golden sty, feeding from silver troughs, and strutting, and spreading his tail, for all the world to admire. But I trust we are about to rise above the mere animal, to the exercise of those faculties that distinguish man as man. God becomes conscious of Himself only in humanity. The supreme good is to be found only in our higher nature; the inner sense does not open till the outer of the mere animal is closed; and it is in that serene quiet only that Nature unveils, and admits us to communion and union.

The Coming Spirit World Evolved from the Spirit Atmosphere, the Result of Cerebration.

We have, I think, yet to discover Man's place in Nature, but in "Evidence as to Man's Place in Nature," Mr. Huxley tells us "The whole analogy of natural operations furnishes so complete and crushing an argument against the intervention of any but what are termed secondary causes, in the production of all the phenomena of the universe, that, in view of the intimate relations between man and the rest of the living world, and between the forces exerted by the latter and all other forces, I can see no excuse for doubting that all are co-ordinated terms of nature's great progression, from the formless to the formed, from the inorganic to the organic, from blind force to conscious intellect and will." As we have seen, I do not recognize blind force anywhere, and the persistence of force shows that in that respect there is no difference between one force and another, either conscious or unconscious. Every atom tends to purpose; then, we have the intelligent but unconscious vital powers; for vital action is not less intelligent than mental, only it goes on unconsciously; we have instinct or sentient intelligence without reasoning, and conscious and reasoning intellect and will, but all are equally caused, all are effects or *second* causes. Purely mental states or conscious volitions, when sufficiently repeated, pass into the unconscious, and all the great laws of nature are probably but the automatic or unconscious will of the Great Supreme. But I did not quote Mr. Huxley to show in what I differed from him, but to show that I recognize fully the great law of evolution. "From the formless to the formed, from the inorganic to the organic," we have the conversion of force or power into sentiency, culminating in "the conscious intellect and will of man;" but as Huxley elsewhere tells us, "Naturalists find man to be no centre of the living world, but one amidst endless modifications of life," and that "present existences are but the last of an immensurable series of predecessors." Undoubtedly man is the highest in the series, but is he to remain so? The aggregate of mind, as it has been passing and repassing during countless ages through living forms, from the monad to man, has been gradually improving in delicacy and intensity of feeling and consciousness, and what may be the next form it may take who can tell? May not the spiritualist theory be merely casting its shadow before? Plants prepare the food for animals, and the elaborate machine of the animal body prepares the food for mind, that is, sentiency and conscious intelligence, and may not this result of cerebration, which has been intensifying for centuries, furnish ground for a new start—for the existence of mind, in an individual form, without all the present cumbrous machinery for the correlation of force? We have a world of spiritual food already prepared, so that there would be no necessity for the old apparatus. If it be true, as is testified by the spiritualists, that hands and arms are now formed in such an atmosphere, who can tell what will be the ultimate effect of will power—for I hold the whole universe to be the effect of will power on certain prepared conditions—as the thought or spirit atmosphere intensifies by the greatly increased action of brain now going on? If such an additional link should ever be added to the chain of intelligence, if such a creation of a new being should ever take place, it will probably be evolved and come into existence, as man did, out of the newly-prepared circumstances and conditions, and not individually representing any previously existing living entity. Such beings would be clairvoyant, would certainly require no railroads, and no electric telegraph, being governed by a law of levitation, rather than of gravitation, and would possess all the powers in a higher degree of which we have only had a glimpse; and cerebration having furnished a sufficient atmosphere and food for their existence, might cease, and the world, with all its increased and increasing beauty, be given up to them. The "spheres," the present abode of spirits, according to the Spiritualists, seem very comfortless regions. But, of course, this is mere speculation. What we have now to do is to investigate and test the abnormal powers surrounding us—to reduce them to law, and thus to pass them on from Man, by whom they have hitherto been only abused, to Humanity, by which they might be used to make the greatest spiritual advance hitherto achieved.

THE END.

APPENDIX.

APPENDIX.

While these sheets have been going through the press, I have received several communications on the subjects under discussion from Mr. H. G. Atkinson, which will be very valuable, I think, to the advanced student in Psychology; I have therefore given them below. They are chiefly in reply to questions by me.

A.—(Page 87.)

The way we speak points to the position of these faculties. I find the seat of judgment behind comparison, and before the sense of Self, and the Will, and the Attention, which is Mental Concentration, a close attendant.

I think, therefore I am. There you have the judging or proper thought faculty, the Eye of the Mind and the sense of the individual personality. Again *I will*, the two organs together again, or 'compare and judge,' the organ of comparison naturally before the judgment or resolution of the forces or elements of the case. The more one reflects on the matter from all directions the more natural and admirable the arrangement seems, and the more clear and absolute necessity for the new organs in question. I hope you will come to see it—though doubtless the matter is most difficult and profound, but it is discovery, and no invention of mine.

The intuition, so to speak of character as with Sir Walter Scott, is really a profound insight or judgment, not mere imitation as in acting, and so thus your observation tallies with mine, and the inner organ above would be raised, as in the case of the protruding eye, from the enlarged organ behind. Then again, these inner powers being essential to life are more protected, being the inner or beneath convolutions, and so the rationale of the matter presents itself on every hand.

Now if the truth and stamp of all is everywhere, all in each part and each in all, as I have said, (See "Letters," p. 256. Trübner and Co.) the inner senses, assuming the ability, could have the truth within itself instead of merely taking up the siftings of a few particulars through the senses channels. Now do you see it all, and the deep sense of the thing, by a glimpse at the reason for the faith that is in me, the offspring of long and patient experimenting, and no one can say I have been anxious to make a vain display; and not for lack of the means to do so, as you, I think, know.

The inner sense is the synthetic power, or formative power and sense, summing-up—all mean the same,—to define, distinguish, abstract, and realise the truth and law. The process itself being instinctive and indefinite to our senses, or only cognizable in the effect and fact.

The *feeling of motion* or *sense of moving*, combines with its neighbour the impulse towards action, sloping towards the destructive and combative impulses. Here we live the busy life, and very much independent of the will. First we have the sense of being, the moi, the Ego—or King; the will we may call prime minister, preceded by the judge, and the impulse or desire of action is the executive. So the mind may find a very pretty simile in a government—in the "Letters" it is likened to a republic, and in fact it is a government or republic, and the simile very complete. This will be a point I shall work out because it will fix the map and plan and principle of the arrangement of the organs and of the faculties in the mind of learners and thinkers, and it is a great thing to exhibit a rational order and reason for that order with an evidently more natural and complete analysis of the component parts of the mind, in their true meaning and relations, all which must be set forth in a very clear manner.

What I have said in the "Letters" was only as a suggestion to aid others in their enquiries, but as they will not inform themselves I must now develop my discoveries and views more fully and in a clear but concise form. If I have been silent it is not from any doubt, but rather in the consciousness of wealth, and that I have made a very great advance in laying the foundation of a true Psychological science. Phrenology as it stood was hardly that, nor was its method sufficient —the very nature of the matter requires other means to aid and correct and complete Gall's discoveries; but it will be accepted again under proper cautions and with the new aids that can now be offered. I cannot however think so little of Gall's method as you infer, when I hold to so much arrived at by that system alone. Do not let there be the slightest misconception upon this. However though the organology be doubted, if I can exhibit a very intelligible order and scheme with an evidently fuller and closer analysis of the faculties than was ever devised before, a great advance will be recognised even by those who remain opposed to phrenology; and we shall show certain fundamental laws of action and reason, that have never been even thought of, and shall be chiefly indebted to mesmerism, by which we have been able to make man an object of experiment as well as of observation. Now if this be true,—and we know that it is so,—there can be no question but that we have discovered one of the greatest and most valuable truths ever revealed to man: the means and power of investigating his own nature. Whatever doubt may be cast upon the discoveries already supposed to have been made, there can be no question as to the immense importance of the means discovered, and of the Psychological laws exhibited in such means. Difficulties of course there are in the application of such means; but the difficulties arise from other new truths discovered not less marvellous and important, such as the power of thought reading, clairvoyance, and the like wonders, but only wonderful from the novelty and rarity—for in truth no fact in nature is more wonderful than another, or really more intelligible. The facts and conditions and laws are all we can know and all we need to know.

All dreaming and other abnormal conditions is like nature experimenting for us, and showing us the way to separate the action of the powers, that we may observe and analyse them better; it is like the opening of a window in the breast, that Momus sighed for; and there is no saying to what extent experiment may reach in extraordinary instances under abnormal conditions. No doubt the faint recurrence of what has occurred in dreams as from another self may cause some persons, with Plato, to fancy they have lived before, and that all we experience is but the recollection of the Past; but we shall now learn what the tricks of the imagination are, and the reason of the opinions at the root of the different schemes of religion and philosophy. A true science of mind can alone bring men to agree upon sure and rational grounds.

I have just read in Mason Good's "Book of Nature," on Sleep, that after studying the opinions on dreaming from the days of Aristotle to our own day he has never met with anything in the least degree satisfactory or capable of unsolving the perplexities in which it lies entangled. "Whence comes to pass," he says, "that ideas can at all exist in the brain during sleep, or that all the *internal* senses are not as much locked-up as the *external* senses," &c., nor could philosophy previous to my discoveries make any better handle of the subject; but when we find there are inner parts of the brain—a more central group pertaining to the internal senses and individualism, the whole is explained and intelligible at once and the difficulty solved for ever, and every condition of dreaming and trance made clear. But what I am writing to you now will not be very intelligible, and seem but as brittle sticks until fully developed and properly bound together in their true correlations.

"It was a dream, and yet it was not all a dream."—*Byron*.

In reply to your question as to whether there is any special action of the inner faculties in dreaming? Ordinary dreaming does not differ from ordinary thinking, though a more partial life under less control from the incomplete relation on account of the sleeping portion; but we must also consider dreaming to be a special condition of mental action since we attain a clear and real-like vision of objects suggested. I paid you a visit in a large handsomely-furnished apartment I imagined you had taken in my dream last night, and saw you and your wife and the pattern and rich colouring of the carpet and all the objects of the room, with as vivid and exact a sense of their reality, and to infinite particulars as what I see about me at this moment. Here then we find the source of the imagination and invention of the thoughts presenting clear and distinct imagery, but which is all very different from our thinking when awake. The sense power or perceptive faculty would seem to have a double face, one towards the sense channel and the real objects perceived, the other towards the inner discerning powers which decide, imagine and invent, and are more specially intuitive; and the imagined objects become pictures, on what I may call the plane or sphere of the senses. In thinking when awake the relation is open between the inner power and the senses, but when these are closed the inner powers are thrown upon other relations and have other resources and channels of communicating without. Thus to reflect and perceive by the mind's eye direct is very different from the reception of impressions of nature by the channel of the senses. Though to judge or reason is as much perception as the sense of a form, a colour, or similitude—in fact, the entire conscious mind is but as a mirror by a congeries of perceptive powers—and even so of the will itself, which is not a power at all but the sense of a power of which it is merely the image and concomitant. But all this is somewhat beside the question,—in a dream a man is in an unbalanced and fragmentary state, and by this disarrangement comes other relations, somewhat as with many tipsy people, or in taking ether. I do not think there is any absolute difference in the action of seeing visions in sleep from seeing objects when awake, because all seeing is by vision, and of which fact the idealist makes the most or rather asserts it to be all and everything; and when we see extraordinary visions or ghosts when awake and in clear daylight we for a time are so far and partly as in a dream, and on which rests those remarkable facts of electro-biology under which you can make another person believe they see whatever you suggest to them, and in many cases lead them by your silent will, cases which throw great light upon the matter of your enquiry, and help to bring Psychology fairly amongst the inductive and experimental sciences — a change coming over the spirit of our dream, or rather a real science founded on material causes and ascertained rules takes the place of mere contentions and metaphysical dreaming. The effects of electro-biology are then similar to the vision in ordinary dreaming, but which though ordinary is yet abnormal as under disjointed and partial condition and in which you may have clairvoyance and direct impressions from without to the inner and central life, and that will occur which so often does occur in sleep, the knowledge of a death taking place at a distance, with a vision of the dying person embodied in their ordinary clothes, or may be in those the sleeper has last seen them wear, or a mere fancy substitute.

Miss Harding's accounts for which remarkable fact by a real spirit, and its spiritual biologising or empressing the seer with its presence, and in the form it chooses, so that even according to those believers what is seen is but a subjective appearance. Then, omitting the belief in the actuality of the presence of a spirit, I agree very closely with the explanation given, and the fact falls in with the general facts of the ordinary action of our minds. Now as the dreamer receives impressions direct to the inner sense so those powers are free to influence others en rapport and induce corresponding dreams, and indeed influence them to an extent we hardly yet suspect and which we may call a mental contagion, and we see the reason of those spiritual epidemics, religious revivals, the spirit-rapping phenomena, and the like. Similar phenomena occurring simultaneously or in close sequence in different localities — so that what occurs more readily in sleep and mesmeric trance when the senses are mostly closed with new relations and conditions of nervous action set up, does occur under favouring and special conditions in the waking state, and hence we have those wonderful records of clairvoyance and of thought-reading by singularly-gifted individuals, such as Swedenborgh and the Swiss historian Zschokke, (See Letters, p. 377,) or in regard to contagious influences, see the case of the Göethe family. — (P. 215.)

Now when we see a vision in broad daylight and clearly have a double action going on, and the inner senses project an image over the place of the ordinary sight, blotting out or covering a part of it, you see how interesting the subject becomes, and that we seem now to be getting to the roots of the difficulty of that which has perplexed the world since men began to think at all: and to deny the possibility of the truth of clairvoyance is but to support those who know the actuality of the fact in the logical conclusion—that being unnatural it must be supernatural. But when our new facts have been well digested we shall find that the phenomena which has astonished and really frightened us at first, take their place under the ordinary laws of our nature better understood, and do not essentially differ from the normal processes of our ordinary life. The colour of the rainbow—the mystic arch in the heavens, puzzled the world for ages; we now know its laws and natural causes; and so it will be with those colours of the mind, that are passed over now as "very strange," or as "supernatural and unaccountable;" but we shall now give a very good account of them and exhibit man's place in nature and the laws by which he is governed, the destiny he is to fulfil, and be able to say with Quitelet—" L'expérience nous apprend dans le fait, avec toute l'evidence possible, ce qui à premiere vue, parait absurd."

The real absurdity is to suppose we could ever attain a knowledge of the laws of the human mind by the only methods that have been followed, and by which no advance has been made though the profoundest intellects have ever been engaged in the pursuit, but with a too high an estimating of the power of logical argumentation, omitting altogether the fundamental facts concerned.

You wish to have some account of the state of the mental faculties during mesmeric sleep. Space will not allow me to enlarge upon this deeply interesting subject, or go into all those marvellous matters to which it relates. I shall therefore attempt no more than just to indicate the general distinguishing characteristic of the state.

"With the mesmeric sleeper and somnambule, we have the brain awake and the sense dead asleep and generally insensible to touch or sound; a pistol fired off at the ear will not produce the least effect; nay you may cut the sleeper to pieces, limb by limb, and he will not awake or be aware of anything going on. I have held a patient's hand and talked to her on indifferent matters while her leg was being amputated, and could not detect the slightest sign of her having any knowledge of the circumstance; but only pinch the little finger of the mesmeriser and she would feel it intensely as of an action upon herself: becoming a perfect response to the condition of the power that had influenced her. There is then a state induced under which, in a certain sense, instead of being imprisoned the powers are loosened, or at least a sensitiveness to impressions set up for which the ordinary conditions of the nervous system are inadequate. In a similar way the patient will read your thoughts and even revive in herself impressions latent in your own brain, or the memory of things long forgotten: or may be able to receive other subtle impressions as they may be directed according to the particular powers and speciality of the case.

"So that we may consider the ordinary senses as rather impediments, or as the veiling of the mental powers to prevent excess and confusion and to utilise the powers to the practical requirements of life. Besides, we must remember the imperfections of the senses and the delusions to which they are all subject, and in all cases it is not by a process of reasoning but by the decision of judgment that the errors are reconciled; reason is but a sort of mental mechanism, whereas judgment is the sense of the result and truth by a higher or thorough perception of the active elements of the particular case. Now the organ of this power is that central intelligent faculty we have called the inner sense, or eye of the mind, as I have described it—it is the judgment seat or tripod on which is seated the high priestess of the 'reasonable soul' and true source of all real genius and what has ever been termed inspiration. And this inner power, together with the conscious power, the sense of identity, and others discovered by me fill and make good the gap and want that has always been pointed out in the phrenological scheme. The entranced person having no sense of the physical world by the senses, or of the existence of his own body, feels perfectly free from all accidents and fears. Hence many a religious delusion and spiritual notion. Now the medium is in a somewhat different position, there being no mesmeriser, but a self-existent or induced semi-trance condition, from the action of the circle, so that the sense or feeling or voice of the inner power is attributed to a spirit; a very natural and necessary delusion under the circumstances. Wanting the control and tie as it were of the mesmeriser the loosened power has a free course in influencing matters without; but this is a question too delicate and complicated to go into at this moment.

"In the last number of the 'Spiritual Magazine' will be found a most interesting case by William Howitt, of a spiritual clairvoyant, who, alluding to the inner sense says, "He in whom this inner sense, this eye of the spirit, has opened, sees those things invisible to others which are in union with him. From the inner sense religions have proceeded, and so many of the apocalypses of the olden and present times." The attendant spirit of Socrates, or voice of warning, was but a seeming inward utterance, or 'still small voice'—from the inner sense—and only look upon the remarkable form of his head in that round swelling protuberance of the higher and central portion of the forehead; a clear phrenological indication in that extraordinary man.

"The greatest geniuses have always more or less partaken of the clairvoyant character, whether poet, painter, or philosopher. Lord Bacon was a clairvoyant, and he curiously relates, and thus delivered himself on the distinction between the ordinary powers of sense and reason and of the higher or farther and fuller powers we are considering:—

"'For though the responses of a divine oracle and of the senses are different, no doubt both in the matter and the mode by which it finds access to the mind; yet the spirit of man which receives both is one and the same, just as different liquors passing through different apertures are received into one and the same vessel, and that part which seems to fall without the division, prophecy, is itself a species of history with the prerogative of deity stamped upon it, of making all time one duration, so that the narrative may anticipate the fact.'

"I would only add the further remark, that those extraordinary powers we are now considering are really not essentially distinct from the ordinary actions of the brain and will be found, and I think I have found them, to be included within the same law; a general law with these exceptional instances: but what has never been done before, cannot be expected to be discovered and revealed by any of the older means and methods. But all we do is natural in its time and place, and distrust or insensibility to what is out of a man's particular line and habitual experience is a law of our nature, and indeed we must confess the matters brought to light do seem very strange and unlikely until investigated. But in fact, being such as they are, if we deny their existence in place of endeavouring to give a rational account of them it can only happen that ignorant people will believe them to be supernatural and cling to them with a blind pertinaciousness and mischievous religious fanaticism.

"I dare say that I often repeat myself in reply to your questions; but that cannot be helped, from the bearing of your enquiries to a particular end."

B.—(Page 90.)

The clairvoyance or other exalted or additional sense or power of the more sensitive to impressions in divers directions must be guided and used as the other powers and ordinary senses are and in no other way—that is, simply as *instrumental* to discovery—and so the abnormal states made to become lights by which to detect the laws of the normal condition, as I have shown and exemplified in the Letters to Miss M.; and just as we use the additional power derived from the telescope which at first professors pertinaciously refused to look into, to see a little farther, or of the microscope, to see a little clearer into that which is before us—otherwise it is merely another condition of dreaming, with sense and nonsense, truth and folly, clear-seeing and illusions commingling fantastically together. The extra sense and power must be also tested as to its truth, speciality and limits, as with all other powers, and cross-questioned as with any foreign or doubtful witnesses in court, by our common senses and previous knowledge and by the result as it shall be made to appear in fact, opposed by other truths and tested in every possible or known way; and just as the ordinary senses are made each to correct each or to witness to each other, so we shall find as in all other matters, that the exceptional phenomena duly weighed and examined will, in the end, exhibit the rule of ordinary action in the reason of the exception. But to wait upon the revelations of clairvoyants, and their grand and pretentious utterances brings you to nothing but a contradictory confusion of ideas—often to what is both extremely beautiful and most true—but to nothing that is super-excellent or actually new, for the somnambule left to itself is in a similar position to the metaphysicians in their subjective waking dreams, each producing a scheme reflecting his imbibed notions and special nature—and after thousands of years of such metaphysical scheming and spinning out of cobwebs, as Bacon calls it, they have come to no agreement, but are going over the same ground in the same contentious and ineffectual way, showing great power and learning but depending upon the light from within with a mistaken estimate of the mind's nature and powers, instead of referring to the real physical causes and facts of objective nature bearing upon the special enquiry, as in every other correctly scientific method of proceeding, for instance, when a somnambule or entranced person is so sensitive that the organs of the brain will respond to the magnetic touch which I discovered to be the fact—and just as the keys of the piano answer to the pressure of the finger, so also another instrument near at hand and in perfect accord will often respond again to the particular note, as the sensitive patient responds or becomes influenced as by a contagion, with the thoughts and feelings or even latent conditions of another *en rapport* with them; and so on, I could recount to you a whole volume of such beautiful and deeply interesting facts in illustration of these profound truths—the most choice and precious lights of philosophy to all future ages—when men have awakened, and ceased to be entranced by their prejudices and pre-conceptions, anticipating in place of interpreting nature—deeming clairvoyance and the like extraordinary powers to be impossible, and yet to know which most astonishing fact as to the limits of the possible in nature they must themselves be possessed of clairvoyance. However what is said by Dr. Buchner, in his "Matter and Force," to be impossible, you and I know to be true, and not very difficult to comprehend either. As to the belief in spirits, the entire history of science and of mankind exhibits a progress of knowledge advancing over spiritual belief. However the modern spiritualist does not mean by spiritual anything supernatural, but that the spirits after passing through the shadow of death are as much a part of nature as before, and the released spirit not essentially different from when enclosed and imprisoned in the body, like a bird in a cage, fretting against the wires, longing to be set free. But the besetting notion of the all glorious nature of spiritual substance and power as contradistinguished from gross *materiality*, when not mere clap-trap is very foolish nonsense, just as when they suppose man degraded by his so-called animal faculties and propensities and the like, I had almost said, insult nature by ignorant and impious sentimentalities to please man's conceit and fancies tending to his own glorification. Whereas the real noble thought, and the noblest perhaps, is in a sense of our own insignificance in the immensity of nature and of powers unknown and beyond our ken. In such intellectual humility the man is most exalted, rising in the calm satisfaction of having conquered his own irrational pride, which may well be designated the vanity of vanities, and whatever we do, let us not be ridiculous but show our superiority in the attainment of knowledge and by rendering a true account of the gift of reason—loving truth in the faith that it ever must conduce to man's highest and noblest inspirations under all life's trials, and the battle we should make from first to last to conquer self.

Whilst this week's *Reader* is before you (May 12th), I would call your attention to the clairvoyance of the celebrated Doltinean, which Mr. Trood endeavours to account for; but if the facts he relates were even possible and true, they would not in the least account for the sight of a ship 400 miles away. To accept such-like explanations would be indeed to strain at a gnat and swallow a camel. Now, Mr. Bottineau declared that strength of eyesight had nothing to do with his observations, and

APPENDIX.   159

he might have added that indeed his eyes had nothing at all to do in the matter; that he perceived by an inner sense that he could not account for. But I think I have accounted for it, and traced the power to its source and seat. The case is so clear and well authenticated that I think you would do well to refer to it; and in presence of such notorious historical evidence, Coleridge wisely remarks that "It is impossible to say whether an 'inner sense' does not really exist in the mind, seldom developed indeed, but which may have a power of presentment. All the external senses have their correspondent in the mind; the eye can see an object before it is distinctly apprehended. Why may there not be a corresponding power in the soul? The power of prophecy might have been merely a spiritual excitation of this dormant faculty."—("Table Talk," vol. 1, pp. 86-7). I do not hold with Coleridge that the exhibition of clairvoyance is from any so-called spiritual excitation of a dormant faculty, but that it may be accounted for, as experiment seems to show, from an extraordinary action of the ordinary faculties under special conditions, by which the 'eye of the mind,' or 'inner sense,' receives impressions independent of the sense channels, and arrives at conclusions without the intervention, or at least without a recognition, of the intellectual process leading to such conclusions, and which is more or less the case with the most of our determinations under ordinary circumstances; and when remarkably displayed, is what we call inspiration, or intuition, or genius; and thus the astonishing facts that men are apt to discredit are but extraordinary after all, and are all to be reduced to a general and uniform law. It is clear that many of the lower animals—bird, beast, and insect—have such impressions from a distance, and are so guided, as we say, by instinct; instances will immediately occur to every one. Then is it hard to suppose that more highly-developed man should under all circumstances be wholly free from such so-called instinct, but which in fact is but another or inner sense set free? The ordinary sense channels, indeed, seem rather to be impediments to avoid confusion and for the selection of special actions, and as a means by which to direct the attention to particular facts or qualities, and may be dispensed with—as, for instance, in the case of the bat with its eyes removed, and yet able to avoid objects even in the dark with equal precision. In fact, we are still confounded by the false notion that the perception is in the organs of the sense. Once quite clear of this error, and the difficulty of understanding the existence of finer sensibilities and higher powers ceases; and we may well feel ashamed of the foolishness of our objections. I cannot too often repeat this: that the course of our enquiries is simply to show that what seems so wonderful and at first to be impossible is really not essentially different from the ordinary action of the mind in its purely normal state.

C.—(Page 120.)

Here we have an undoubted case of clairvoyance, happening to a learned divine and leader of the great High Church party. A man still living in our midst and able to answer for the truth of the statement, and which is not denied. And how does the matter stand? There is certainly no actual bodily presence such as the ordinary senses could take cognisance of, but an impression by the passing off of a certain vital nervous force from the dying man, affecting the inner sense of one in sufficient rapport with his special condition, and from which inner sense and abstract self is projected on the sense plain as it were—the image of the person in question, and even to an echo of the sense within in the sound and utterance as of a voice, and conveying an intelligent meaning, the intelligence of the death and of the lie; but the truth conveyed mingling with the particular convictions of the recipient in his belief of Hell. In this we may read an analysis of the Psychical fact and the anatomy of ghosts,—there is a clear impression on the inner sense from a force without upon one in sympathetic relations or rapport with the distant dying person, and an embodiment from such impression, but with a colouring and fashioning by the special conviction of the recipient; a fiction founded on fact; with the vision and all just as in a dream, like the fancy when it plays tricks with fact in our waking moments, and really there is very little difference, all happening under one and the same law.

No doubt Dr. Pusey believes that he has seen a spirit bringing him immediate intelligence of Hell, and the spiritualists would claim him as a medium—only they do not believe in a Hell, but only in a gradual progression, and that sin is simply imperfection, under universal law—at least such is the "inspired" doctrine of that marvellously eloquent lady Miss Hardinge, whose impressions and promptings—(when in a "semi-trance,") from the inner sense she takes to be a spirit—are really replete with profound learning and most admirable sense, come by it how she may; from her own very excellent nature under certain abnormal conditions I believe; and that she is perfectly serious in her conviction that she is inspired by a spirit. Men who are so ready to deem all those who differ from them to be insincere impostors would do well to remember that in such judgment they do but reflect their ignorance, stupidity, and own unenviable qualities and bad nature. I say then, "*Judge not, lest ye be judged.*"

It often happens to me as I walk along the streets that I imagine I see a friend approaching, but on nearer inspection I see it is some one

APPENDIX. 161

else not having the least resemblance to the friend supposed; but immediately after, perhaps within a minute, I do really meet the friend I had just supposed I had seen as it were covering the figure of the stranger; and I never have made the mistake except when it has been followed by the presence of the friend supposed. The explanation is that you have a real impression from the approaching friend whilst not yet in sight—an impression taken up by the inner sense and which impression is projected and embodied upon the first form that approaches, somewhat as forms in the dusk will shape themselves in accordance with imaginary fears, in fact we exhibit for the time a similar power to the somnambule and clairvoyant who has such a sensitive impression of the physical condition of the mesmeriser even when he is at a distance as to produce a reflexion of his thoughts and even latent memories.

I have just seen a Ghost!—I was thinking of friends just dead as reported to me by Miss M., buried amidst the spring's primroses, and turning my face to the window I saw on the opposite side a woman carrying a basket on her head, full of flowers, (common enough now in London,) oh! so beautiful, with a mass of yellow primroses in the midst, I thought I had never seen any look so bright and beautiful. I turned my head away but for an instant, I looked again, and lo there was no woman or flowers at all—It was just a vision as in a dream, occurring maybe from having a cold and liver out of order and some head-ache, but there was the vision sure enough or seeming appearance, even brighter than reality, and in the midst of sunshine. I think I told you that I have marvellous visions of objects in my sleep, with every minute particle and variety of object as clear as possible, and palpable as real objects seen in daylight, and I have recalled the clear impression in every minute particular and delicate difference of shade and colour, and painted it in the morning. Now does not all this open a window for us and give us some light into the inner sense and Psychology of the mind and as depending on physical conditions—similar to the effect under electro-biology? Indeed our ordinary perceptions are not essentially different, being entirely visionary though corresponding with the object producing the impression, and this again causing the vision or perception much as a picture represents its subject, and so of the vital photography and reflected imagery of the mind we call seeing.

M

162   APPENDIX.

Shakspeare was right about the causes, the indwelling upon thought and "heat-oppressed brain," and the action and reflex is from the mirror of the sense power just as when the sense channels are closed by sleep, and yet the interior faculties awake in the dream, with the sense power reversed as it were and producing all that inner and other world by remembering and reflection — a mere pictorial exhibition with occasional intuitive presentiments and clairvoyance — such as we produce under mesmerism and by which we do but produce artificially what occurs under certain conditions in special subjects in the normal state; I mean we create no new faculty or power, but only produce conditions under which the ordinary power may act in an extraordinary way; indeed in mesmerism we have the power of experimenting on man and mind as the chemist and electrician deals with inanimate matter. Any one who does not see the deep importance of such a power must be either very ignorant or very stupid.

———

In regard to the slight and somewhat doubtful instances I have given to you by way of explaining the general nature of visual illusions, I must again repeat that in gathering facts by which to arrive at the true laws of vision we cannot be too curious in recording exceptional and seeming trivial instances, or what may be called deviating instances, under unusual conditions — when as it were you catch nature out of bounds. Foolish critics have pointed ridicule at me for saying this, nevertheless the method applies to all science, and the history of every science will exhibit the truth and value of the principle, but which applies with infinitely greater force in regard to the study of the more complex and varied phenomena of mind, whose mysterious and hidden truths have escaped detection by all the means and methods and modes of demonstration hitherto practised. The fact is, man himself has been regarded as an exceptional instance in nature, degraded in one sense as a creature incapable of attaining any excellence of itself, and on the other hand exalted into a free agent and almost supernatural being, apart and essentially different from other living creatures, so that the real man has remained unrevealed in his true nature to this hour. But we must now consider man as a natural body, producing individual effects according to particular laws in harmony with general and universal principles, and whilst omitting none of the facts concerned we must be careful to avoid

APPENDIX. 169

hasty generalising, a glaring instance of the folly of which may be noticed in Berkeley's celebrated theory of vision founded upon the appearance of the rising moon—he had made a guess at what looked like the truth and never followed up the inquiry into all the circumstances of the case, never, in fact, cross-questioned his witnesses; but indeed his entire theory and argument is fallacious throughout. And again, he inconsistently denies the existence of the material external world whilst dogmatically insisting on a universal immaterialism and world of spirits —not seeing that the sauce for the goose is sauce for the gander. If I were dying I think my last words of admonition to the student in Psychology should be—look out for the exceptional instances, and for similar facts occurring in other creatures and under different conditions; but there is nothing new in this, which was urged with so much force and sagacity by Bacon; but proud man has scorned the application to his own nature, and yet it is a principle that none with a genius for scientific enquiry would for a moment dispute, and is in fact no more than a very general rule which may be exemplified as I have said in all and each of the sciences from the extraordinary instances in regard to the motions of the planets to the trifling action of the Frog's leg, that in a natural sequence resulted in the Electric Telegraph—the most wonderful achievement of modern science. So let no one despair of magnificent and useful results from the study of Psychology after a true method and similar line of investigation. But Psychology must be based on Physiology, must be regarded as a physical science—a science of phenomena traced to their material and real causes, or it will end as it has ever done, in mere disputation, and in fact would be no science at all.

For if a tree be cut away from its roots, no wonder if it shall perish, and there be no further growth. Metaphysical schemes always remind me of the bunches of wild flowers that children gather in the fields, each declaring that his own bunch is the best; but alas! they are all of little value, and wither in the poor children's hot hands ere they reach home. And so it is with those children of thought, the metaphysicians, who take up the flowers of the mind irrespective of the causes that produce them, the source from which they emanate, the roots from which they develop, the soil in which they grow, the atmosphere by which they are surrounded and light that is shed upon them, and much besides that is disregarded, and with a proud exalting of the unassisted power of the human mind, far beyond the fact—unmindful of the faulty nature and inequality of the mirror and imperfections of the instrument searching into its own nature. And as a child in regard to its parents, the metaphysician is necessarily unconscious of the causes of the phenomena he reflects upon, and hence insensibly passes over the true reason of the differences and speciality of men's nature and of

APPENDIX.

the opinions they incline to on account of such differences. The whole aim of science is a search into causes to ascertain on what effects depend and the laws by which they are governed, and the entire relations and correlations in the analogy of knowledge, in those general laws which link the phenomena together in the eternal and universal chain of existence, and the uniform rule, since all truth is necessary truth so far as like causes must always produce like effects, or they would not be like, but something else.

Metaphysicians are aptly compared in that valuable periodical the *Reader* to the Kilkenny cats, that fought and ended in eating each other up, leaving only their tails behind; for metaphysicians are pretty much engaged, each in destroying the argument of his opponent, and the very universe and Great Cause inherent therein is lost in the argument between them and reduced to the merest shadow, without the slightest shame or remorse on their part; so that the reviewer pointedly and justly remarks that "the ground has been cleared, and he who can prove the existence of God will inherit it." Now Mr. Mill, after feasting upon Hamilton, has in turn been gobbled up himself, leaving only a metaphysical tail behind, in the form of a remarkable expression, namely, "Permanent Possibilities": but what is in a name with only folly and illogical reasons behind it, and at the end of it? For a very clear refutation and lucid exposure of which folly see an admirable little work published by Newby, called "Odd Bricks," by a very acute reasoner and learned friend of mine, who goes into such questions con amore — having a special gift for logical reasoning and no theory of his own to defend, which is a blinding influence with most men, Mr. Mill certainly not excluded, whose ignorance of Race, and inability to discern the value of physiology as the necessary and essential basis of mental science, is most lamentable, and from his reputation and authority now most obstructive and mischievous.

www.ingramcontent.com/pod-product-compliance
Lightning Source LLC
Chambersburg PA
CBHW020302170426
43202CB00008B/464